"Inspired by the ornaments tha̶... ...
Donna Amidon skillfully brings to life the promises and prophecies in
the Old Testament that point to Christ from creation to his advent. As
you journey with Donna, you travel with an insightful and knowledge-
able guide who provides rich commentary concerning the people and
events that foreshadow the coming of Christ. Along the way, she lays
a firm foundation, revealing the bigger story of Jesus and our personal
relationship with him. You will find *Tracing His Promise* to be a hope-
filled journey proclaiming the invaluable truths that God is with us
and Jesus is all in all."

—CYNTHIA HEALD, Bible teacher and author of the popular
Becoming a Woman Bible study series

"*Tracing His Promise* bridges the gap between ancient history and modern faith in a transformative exploration of Scripture. With each page,
readers will discover the richness of the Old Testament and a deeper
understanding of Jesus's presence and promise throughout. This book
is more than just a study; it's an invitation to encounter Jesus in a fresh,
profound, and life-changing way. Amidon's heartfelt storytelling and
insightful reflections invite readers to explore the depths of ancient
narratives and discover their profound relevance to contemporary
faith."

—DR. STEPHEN CUTCHINS, senior pastor at FBC North Augusta, SC,
and author of *Prove It*

"*Tracing His Promise* is a powerful, biblically grounded study that reveals profound connections between Old Testament Scripture and
the Messiah who was born in Bethlehem and is undeniably Jesus.
Throughout the study, Amidon illuminates for the reader the significance of events, prophecies, and people of Old Testament times—not
only how they relate directly to Jesus's birth but also how Jesus was
present from the beginning of it all. Amidon engages readers through

thought-provoking questions, impactful illustrations, and deep insight. She invites families to incorporate the Jesse Tree into their Christmas traditions and provides creative ideas and printable ornaments. Amidon's passion is evident at every turn of the page while she helps her readers make golden-nugget connections hidden in plain sight. This study is unique and impactful! Don't miss it!"

—DORIS SWIFT, host of *Fierce Calling*, speaker, and author of
Surrender the Joy Stealers

"*Tracing His Promise*—containing the meticulous research and insights of Donna Amidon—is an extraordinary resource for all who seek truth about Jesus Christ. The author's knowledge of Scripture and history and her personal application of the Bible will be an inspiration for all readers. It is a privilege to recommend such a unique and timely book."

—ALEX MCFARLAND, apologist, educator, broadcaster

"Donna reveals the Jesus Christ of the New Testament in the stories of the Old Testament where he is concealed. She brings this to light in a way that is not only exciting and real but in a way that shows us the privilege we have to apply his truth to our lives and the situations we face daily. Her testimonies of how she has walked this out are amazingly applicable to each of us. I'm very excited to begin *Tracing His Promise* in our own church groups to enable us to walk more like Christ, by his Spirit. A must-read for those seeking to know him more."

—STEWART FARLEY, pastor of Rhema Christian Center

"I am grateful that Donna wrote *Tracing His Promise*, which is a book that can help anyone deepen their understanding of the Bible. This book beautifully uncovers the presence and person of Jesus Christ in both the Old and New Testaments, guiding readers to encounter our Savior in a profound and intimate way. Whether you are a new Christian or a mature believer in Christ, *Tracing His Promise* can be a valuable resource to help you grow in your knowledge of Scripture and develop greater intimacy and consistency in your walk with Jesus."

—JASON JIMENEZ, founder and president of Stand Strong Ministries and best-selling author of *Hijacking Jesus*

"What I loved about this book is the way Donna helped me see Jesus in an even bigger way. In her down-to-earth way, she helps us see Christ as present and powerful from the beginning pages of Scripture all the way through. This book invites you to experience his presence and power in your own life. I can't recommend it more highly."

—BRANDON SAMUEL, senior pastor of The Chapel, Richmond, VA

"The Bible is a story of God's creation, our rebellion, and God's decision to send his Son, Jesus, into the world to restore it. The prophecies throughout the Old Testament predict Jesus's first coming. That's what Donna has captured in this book. She shows not only the astounding unity of God's Word but also the Father's deep and abiding love for us through Jesus. I pray the church, Jesus's bride, can use it to experience God's eternal love in greater depth."

—DAVID CHADWICK, pastor of Moments of Hope Church and author of *Moving Beyond Anxiety*

"*Tracing His Promise* is thoughtful and in-depth about who Jesus is—from the beginning of creation to the cradle to the grave—and how we experience life with him today. It also includes an interactive way to share these truths with your kids and grandkids by making Christmas ornaments. I'm so thankful Donna Amidon took the time to define the bigger story of Jesus for us and included thoughtful ways to share his story!"

—ARNIE COLE, chief executive officer at Back to the Bible and research and development director at Spiritual Fitness Data Center

TRACING
HIS
Promise

Understanding the Bigger Story of Jesus
and What That Means for Us

D O N N A   A M I D O N

Cataloging-in-Publication Data is available from the Library of Congress.

ISBN 978-0-8254-4816-4, print
ISBN 978-0-8254-6998-5, epub
ISBN 978-0-8254-6997-8, Kindle

Printed in the United States of America

24 25 26 27 28 29 30 31 32 33 / 5 4 3 2 1

CONTENTS

CONTENTS

INTRODUCTION

When you think of Jesus, what image comes to mind? Is he a tender baby in a manger, a compassionate man on a cross, the reigning King of heaven?

What if Jesus is even greater than you imagined? What if there's more to his story and its connection to our lives than we ever dreamed?

The invitation was simple—an ornament exchange for women. Being neither crafty nor having time to spare, I would have normally brushed off the idea of exchanging homemade ornaments. But for some reason, I said yes. Little did I know I'd be introduced to Jesus in a way I'd never experienced before.

As part of the exchange, I made twenty-five ornaments resembling ancient scrolls. The night before the exchange, I dug out paper, glue, and a box of matches. There I sat, rolling strips of paper and burning the edges for an aged effect. *What have I gotten myself into?*

After the exchange, everyone who'd participated had a set of twenty-five ornaments representing twenty-five stories that collectively traced Jesus and his promise through the Old Testament. I still remember carrying the shoebox of ornaments home that day, not realizing how these simple decorations and the stories they represented would transform our family's Christmas and how we viewed Jesus in the Old Testament.

Once home, I opened the box and looked through the ornaments. I picked up a small slingshot with smooth stones, representing David, the shepherd boy to whom God promised a Son with an eternal throne. I cradled a delicate lamb ornament, representing the Passover—an event that foretells the coming Christ like no other. I picked up a fiery furnace ornament, symbolizing not only the incredible test of Shadrach, Meshach, and Abednego but a reminder of the glorious *fourth* man in the fire.

That Christmas our family used these twenty-five ornaments to create our own Jesse Tree—a decorative tree that tells of the coming Christ. Beginning December 1 and going through Christmas, we added one ornament to the tree each day and shared the stories with our children.

During that first season using the Jesse Tree, something stirred in my heart. Though I had gone to church my whole life and was in seminary, God's redemptive plan came alive not only in my mind but in my heart *and* eyes. I loved seeing the connections between the Old and New Testaments. I savored how each event, story, and prophecy pointed to Jesus and his birth in Bethlehem—brushstrokes in a grand painting of love and redemption.

More than that, I realized that Jesus was not just a fulfillment of prophecy, nor was his life confined to the crimson letters of the New Testament. He was there—in the beginning—with God. He had been there all along.

It's been fourteen years since that first ornament exchange. In that

INTRODUCTION

time I've had the joy of using the ornaments year after year to teach my children about the promise of Christ. I'll admit—some years have gone better than others. We've had missing and broken ornaments, arguments and meltdowns over whose turn it was to hang that day's ornament.

But despite the chaos and imperfection, the investment paid off. I now see in my children an understanding of Scripture and an invaluable love for God. When Christmas stress levels soar, as they typically do, I breathe deeply with the anticipation of pulling out the ornaments and reflecting on the promised Christ with my family. It's a time when our hearts connect not just with each other but with something greater— someone greater.

Several years ago I'd been praying about a fall study for the ladies at my church. Weeks passed with no clear direction. However, everything changed one morning when my ten-year-old daughter and I were in the kitchen discussing her favorite subject at the time—her dreams of one day having a family.

Without giving it much thought, I asked, "Charity, when you're a mom, will you do the Jesse Tree with your kids?"

With a sparkle in her eye, she said, "Yes!"

Charity's enthusiastic response ignited something deep within me. I began dreaming about what it would be like for women and families in our church to experience the joy of the Jesse Tree. I envisioned women's hearts coming alive as they understood the bigger story of Jesus and God's brilliant plan to save.

That fall I wrote a Bible study for the women at our church. Beginning

INTRODUCTION

with creation, we walked together through the Old Testament story and traced the promises and events leading to Christ's birth. The women loved discovering the richness of the Old Testament and how it connects to the New Testament. They began inviting their sisters, moms, and friends. Their faith blossomed as their understanding deepened.

One woman shared that when she taught her grandson of Abraham's willingness to sacrifice his only son, he replied, "Grandma, this is like a movie trailer for when Jesus would come and die on the cross for our sins!"

Another mom stopped me in my neighborhood. With tears of joy, she shared how, up to that point, Christmas had been about Santa and presents. But now her family was experiencing the joy of placing Jesus center stage.

As I've listened to women's responses, woven through each story is the profound joy of understanding Scripture and knowing Jesus in a new and transforming way. It's more than just information—it's about seeing his extraordinary promise intersect with everyday lives.

And now that Bible study from seven years ago has become the book you're holding in your hands.

Over the next few weeks, we'll see Scripture in a new light. Beginning with Genesis, we'll walk through twenty-five stories, tracing Christ from creation to Bethlehem's cradle.

Let me pause and say I've been where you may be when it comes to reading the Old Testament. I wanted to understand the Scriptures, but they felt overwhelming. I questioned God's ways and wondered why life felt so challenging. What difference would reading the Old

Testament make in my daily life? To sit down and study it, especially as a mom with kids to wrangle, seemed a hill too hard to climb without guarantee of a practical application.

But today begins something new. Together we'll walk the rewarding journey of understanding the Old Testament stories as catalysts of hope for our hearts and encouragement to our steps. We'll replace feelings of brokenness with trust in God's bigger story for our lives. We'll grasp that his overarching plan—then and now—always works for good despite the disappointments and delays.

And don't worry. We won't be adding to Scripture or looking for things that aren't there. In fact, our study will be straight from Scripture, and many of the stories may be familiar to you. But here's the most exciting part: our hearts will ignite as we experience the Old Testament through the lens of the coming Christ. As a beautiful bonus, each story has a corresponding ornament you can share with your family during the Christmas season. (See appendix A.)

Whether or not you incorporate the Jesse Tree as a family tradition, my prayer is that *Tracing His Promise* will help you understand Jesus in the Old Testament and that these twenty-five stories will have the same lasting impact on you as they have had on me.

My yes to that ornament exchange launched my life and family in an incredible direction, and I'm thrilled you have said yes to this study.

Here are some things to note about this book:

- *Tracing His Promise* **is interactive.** Grab a cup of coffee and something to write with, and interact with the study. Most of us have busy schedules and busy brains. We'll benefit from slowing down to take it in.

INTRODUCTION

- **Each section highlights a different segment of Old Testament history.** We will cover a total of twenty-five events, prophecies, and people that point to Jesus's coming—most of which come from the Old Testament.

- **You can go at your own pace.** You can use *Tracing His Promise* as a daily reading plan for twenty-five days or as a study spread out over seven weeks. With a group, I've found that corresponding the seven sections with seven weeks works well. Do what works best for you.

- **This book is not just for the Advent season or for moms with kids at home.** *Tracing His Promise* is an inspiring, standalone study of Jesus in the Old Testament.

- **Each day includes a "Questions" section, which is a space to write your thoughts about that day's lesson.** Refer to these pages if you hang the ornaments. You'll be so happy you kept notes!

- **Appendixes with more information and inspiration are included in the back of the book.** The appendixes provide what you need to begin your own Jesse Tree tradition, including a link for printable ornaments, tips on hosting an ornament exchange, and fun facts about how the Jesse Tree began. For extra resources and creative ideas, visit www.donnaamidon.org/tracinghispromise.

Whether you've walked with Christ for years or are taking your first steps, you're in the right place. My prayer is that your heart will come alive as you discover the Old Testament is not a book of antiquated stories and isolated events. Rather, it is *one* brilliant story revealing Jesus and his coming.

INTRODUCTION

From Genesis to Jesus's birth in Bethlehem, we'll not only experience the richness of the Old Testament, but we'll also see Christ woven into the tapestry of the stories. And as we see Jesus in the Old Testament, I pray it propels you into a lifetime of seeing him in your life.

Love and prayers,

Donna

 Scan this code for more information and additional resources.

EMBRACING A BIGGER VIEW
OF
Jesus

Day 1

CHRIST IN CREATION

Read Genesis 1:1–3; Colossians 1:16–18.

When my kids were little, all the craze among moms was about adding secret ingredients to food to make it healthier. I attended moms' groups where women would pass around ziplock bags packed with pureed cauliflower and black beans, claiming it was the best-kept secret to their cookie and brownie recipes.

I was skeptical until my mom called one day to share her latest discovery.

EMBRACING A BIGGER VIEW OF JESUS

"You won't believe this," she said. "If you mix sweet potatoes and peanut butter, it makes the perfect spread for crackers!"

Okay, I thought. *Why not?* After the call, I mixed the magical spread.

My daughter heard me rummaging in the kitchen and raced to the table. I casually placed the plate of crackers in front of her. And Charity, our adventurous eater, grabbed the cracker and took a big bite of the peanut butter–sweet potato spread. She paused and, almost singing her response, cried, "Mmmmm! Chocolate!"

Trying to keep a straight face and not explode with laughter, I replied, "Oh. Um, great. I'm glad you like it."

Within seconds she gobbled up the plate of "chocolaty" crackers. A mom win for sure!

What still makes me chuckle about that afternoon is that even though I had mixed sweet potatoes and peanut butter, every one of Charity's little taste buds squealed *chocolate.*

What Charity thought was true was *not* true. What she believed was one thing was, in reality, something else.

Let me ask you, Have you ever thought that something you *believed* was true may not actually be true?

More specifically, have you ever thought your view of Jesus may not capture the fullness of who he truly is?

Charity's story illustrates how easily our thoughts can lead to false conclusions. And because our minds can be so convincing, we can fall into the trap of living by something we think is true, rather than what really is.

This leads me to the heart of our journey together. When you think of Jesus, what comes to mind? When you picture him, what do you see?

Is he a baby in a manger? A man on a cross? The King of heaven?

Are his arms folded in frustration or open for embrace? Is he stern and stoic, or does he have a smile on his face?

> ## When you think of Jesus, what comes to mind?

Today and over the next few weeks, I'm going to paint a picture of Jesus that will astound you—he is far more than a man, a gifted teacher, or a powerful prophet. Together we'll unveil the greatness of who he is and how that transforms our lives.

And our starting point may be a surprise to you. We're not on the dusty streets of Jerusalem or by a manger in Bethlehem. We begin at *creation*, where Christ is.

You may wonder, *Why creation? Why not study the miracles of Jesus, like when he turned water into wine?*

Why? Because a miracle happened long *before* water turned to wine that is far more profound. It's when Christ turned darkness into light, chaos into order, and nothing into something.

EMBRACING A BIGGER VIEW OF JESUS

It's when he created all things, the first miracle of our Savior.

Genesis 1:1–2 says, "In the beginning, God created the heavens and the earth. . . . And the Spirit of God was hovering over the face of the waters." In these opening verses, we see God the Father and God the Spirit active in creation.

However, embedded in the creation story is a profound truth the apostle Paul revealed regarding Christ: "For by him all things were created, in heaven and on earth, visible and invisible, whether thrones or dominions or rulers or authorities—all things were created through him and for him. And he is before all things, and in him all things hold together" (Col. 1:16–17).

Incredible, isn't it? Here we see Christ, the second person of the Trinity, active in creation and at creation.[1] In just two verses, Paul unveiled Christ's supremacy like no other passage in the Bible:

- Christ *created* all things.
- All things are *for him*.
- He is *before* all things.
- He *holds together* all things.

For the church at Colossae, Paul knew a higher and true view of Christ was needed to counter the false teachers of his day. And for you and me, a fresh perspective is needed as well. Why? Because I'm convinced we don't see Jesus as he truly is.

Our culture, consumed by self-absorption and digital distraction, has a way of elevating man and diminishing the greatness of God.

Not only that, we have an adversary at work, subtly twisting our perception of who Jesus is. He makes us question God's goodness, which chips away at our faith, leaving us with a God who is distant, impersonal, and beyond reach—descriptions no truer than the chocolate my daughter thought she was eating.

But when you and I know—*really* know—who Jesus is, our lives look radically different. Our affection centers on Christ. And when challenges come, rather than unraveling in worry or carrying the burden on our own, we can rise above situations and radiate peace.

Why? Because Christ sees all, knows all, is before all things, and holds all things together. That's what gave Paul confidence, and it's what anchors our souls as well.

For the rest of today, we'll dive into Paul's four statements and expand our understanding of Christ—the greatness of who he is and the magnitude of his glorious invitation to know him.

Christ Created All Things

After speaking at a conference, I saw a band member heading straight for me, cell phone in hand and a smirk on his face. Shifting his weight side to side and holding his phone in the air, he announced, "I fact-checked you tonight!"

"Really?" I asked, trying to act like this happened every day. "What did you check?"

"I checked what you said about our universe. I didn't believe you. But you were right!"

My message that night had been on worship. I had displayed an image of the Milky Way galaxy and explained we're viewing a part of our universe that contains over four hundred *billion* stars.[2] Then I shared that the speck of light in the Milky Way that we call home is not just the earth. It's our entire solar system. Not only that, scientists believe each one of the four hundred billion stars is like our sun, having at least one or two of its own orbiting planets.[3]

Apparently, the band member believed me to that point. It was my next comment that had him grabbing for his phone.

I explained that if we began at one side of the Milky Way and traveled to the other at the speed of light—186,000 miles per second[4]—it would take a hundred thousand *years* to cross. If that isn't enough, scientists once believed the Milky Way was the only galaxy. But now they know the Milky Way is one of billions—yes, billions—of existing galaxies.[5]

Think of this. When you and I gaze into the night sky, beyond what we see are *billions* of galaxies, with each galaxy comprising millions, or more often, billions of stars. And these billions of galaxies have billions of stars that likely have planets orbiting them. Even now.[6]

Our creation is massive. Our Creator is masterful.

Day 1 | Christ in Creation

Here's what you and I can't forget. The same God who created these billions of galaxies is the God we worship, the one we sing songs to. The one who hears us when we pray and answers our cries.

He's the God who sees our stories and cares for the concerns of our lives. He is in it all, and he is Lord of all.

Do you ever think we unknowingly limit the greatness of God in our minds, living as if our struggles are bigger than our Savior? Or do you ever think there's more to knowing and trusting God than we've experienced?

If God created everything at a size and complexity that surpasses our understanding, can't we trust him to watch over the things that seem so big and complex? Can't we trust him to hold them together and see us through? Can't we believe he's orchestrating everything—even the unseen details?

The answer is a resounding yes!

Christ Is Before All Things

Paul said Christ created all things, and "he is before all things" (Col. 1:17).

I find this fascinating. We can't go back to a certain point and say, "This is when Christ began," because Christ is eternal. If we were to go back in time, our journey would take us to the first day of creation. And there we would find Christ because he has *always* been. He never began.

Let's just take that in for a moment.

How does Christ's eternal nature impact you and me? I'll illustrate using the idea of a parade. When you or I watch a parade, we experience events one at a time, just like we experience our lives one day at a time.

But because Christ is eternal—bound by neither time nor space—he sees things differently. We could think of his perspective like that of someone in the Goodyear blimp or a drone hovering above, viewing every aspect of the parade *at the same time.*

It's a different perspective. A perspective that sees the whole picture at once.

And for you and me, this aspect of Christ's eternal nature should move us not only to marvel, but it can also be an incredible comfort. Why? Because he has a perspective we do not have.

He knows your tomorrow. He sees the future of your marriage, kids, and career. He knows the results of the medical tests you just had and what the doctor will say at your next appointment. He knows how the judge will rule the court case that has you losing sleep. He sees the entire trajectory of your life and the lives of those you love.

He knows all and sees all, and he is there.

Best of all, because he sees all, he knows what's best. He knows if you should say yes to the career opportunity or wait. He knows if the neighborhood you are exploring is right for your family. He knows the best school for your children and church home for your family.

And because he knows, we can trust him with his gentle nudges and whispers to our hearts. He knows what's coming. He loves us, and he is there.

All Things Were Created for Him
Paul said that "all things were created through him and for him" (Col. 1:16).

Day 1 | Christ in Creation

A few years ago, I received a Coach handbag as a Christmas gift. As much as I prefer simplicity, carrying something so posh on my shoulder was quite a boost to the ol' ego. But to my surprise, within a few months the leather straps frayed. After some research online, I raced off to the mall for my warranted replacement.

I sauntered into the boutique, beaming with my Coach bag positioned proudly on my shoulder. The woman at the counter greeted me with a warm smile, and after I explained my situation, she politely took my bag.

Within seconds her expression turned sour. She looked at me and said, "I'm sorry. I can't help you."

"But the website indicated—"

"I'm sorry. I cannot help you. This is *not* a Coach bag."

I gulped. "*Not* a Coach bag?"

She showed me what the real marks of a Coach bag include and how mine fell sadly short. I'll never forget what she said next in her matter-of-fact tone: "We only value originals, not imitations. This bag is of little value."

I still remember the sinking feeling of frustration and embarrassment. And yet what stayed with me more than the awkward moment at the counter was the unforgettable lesson I learned that day: Originals have value. Imitations have limitations.

How does this connect to Christ in creation? Colossians says we are made *by* Christ and *for* Christ. "For by him all things were created . . . [and] all things were created through him and for him" (v. 16). The same God who formed the billions of galaxies and holds every star in place is the same God who formed you—that you would live *for him*.

Originals have value.
Imitations have limitations.

Have you ever considered that everything in your life is for him? The children you're raising, the spouse you're loving, the talent you're developing, the friendships you're pursuing, the business you're growing. All for him.

What if we have it backward? What if we've forgotten—or never realized—that we were created to live for God, not self? What if we're experiencing limited joy because we've made life more about pleasing ourselves and others, rather than pleasing him?

My imitation handbag had limited value because it was pretending to be something it was not. And if we're not careful, we can get caught in the trap of imitating others and limit ourselves from the great plan God has for us.

Paul said we are made *by* Christ and *for* Christ. Our job is not to strive and strain, compulsively compare, or be someone we're not. Our purpose is different. God has called you to be the incredible you he's created you to be and to live every day *for him*. He has a purpose for you and everything your life touches.

Christ Holds Together All Things

On this first day together, the apostle Paul has expanded our understanding of Jesus. We've seen Jesus is before all things, he created all things, and all things—including you and me—are made for him.

Day 1 | Christ in Creation

Of the statements from Colossians, this fourth and final phrase is unique, as it reveals something of the past and gives a glimpse into an ongoing activity of Christ. Colossians 1:17 says, "In him all things hold together." The book of Hebrews echoes this by saying Jesus "upholds the universe by the word of his power" (1:3). What a thought!

Whether the smallest particle in an atom or the billions of galaxies suspended in space, Jesus holds them all together. Nothing is outside his command. *Nothing.*

Here's something we can tuck into our hearts. If Christ, the Creator of all things, holds all things together, how much more will he hold you and me? How much more does he watch over the matters of your life and mine? How much more does he care for the things that concern us?

How much more can we trust him?

You may be like me and confess that sometimes trust can feel challenging. We want to believe God yet wonder why life can be so difficult. We desire to trust God in hard times, but our faith becomes faint, and we stumble more than soar.

So how do we trust? How do we depend on God and not ourselves?

The psalmist David provided a profound answer that brings us back to the heart of our journey.

> *Those who know your name put their trust in you,*
> *for you, O Lord, have not forsaken those who seek you.*
> *(Ps. 9:10)*

Catch the connection. As we *know* him, we will *trust* him.

Know him. Not just who we think he is or perceive him to be. Not what we've assumed or been told by our culture. Rather, we must cling to who he truly is. And as the psalmist said, when we know him, we will trust him. As we seek him, we will not be forsaken.

Beautiful.

I've had some people say that knowledge doesn't equal trust. And I'd agree. We all know people we don't trust. And yet here lies the profound beauty of our journey. As we know God, we will trust him because we'll discover the perfection of his character, his love, and his ways.

Through knowing him, we'll come to understand he has an all-encompassing perspective from which he scripts a huge, glorious story for us and those we love. As we discover him, the fears and uncertainties that have bound us will be replaced with the peace, confidence, and trust that God loves us, sees our story, and has a good plan. Most of all, when we know him we will be convinced of the most treasured of truths: he is with us.

Truth and Trust

I'm convinced our journey to know Jesus is one of the best decisions we can make. But it's not just another spiritual act to accomplish or box to check. We do it to align our life with his plan and to live for him.

I'm on this journey, and I hope you'll join me as well. It's a path of peace the world longs for and a joy that surpasses the best the world can offer. It comes as we know his name and walk in a joy-filled relationship of trust.

Christ made all things.
He is before all things.
All things are for him.
He holds together all things.

Questions

Of the four descriptions we see in Colossians, which one speaks most significantly to you? In what way?

- Christ made all things.
- He is before all things.
- All things were made for him.
- He holds together all things.

Does knowing the greatness of God (galaxies, stars, planets) change how you approach him in worship? How does it change how you pray?

How can the illustration of the parade offer peace for what is ahead?

Imitations have limitations. Do you find yourself swayed by others when it comes to your beliefs, actions, words, or achievements?

What is a situation in your life where it comforts you to know God holds all things together?

JESSE TREE

If you will be creating a Jesse Tree, what is something you want to remember about Christ in creation?

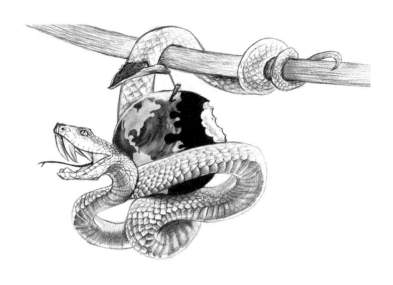

Day 2

MAN'S SIN, GOD'S PROMISE

Read Genesis 3:1–24; 1 John 4:4.

I still remember the morning I was cleaning the kitchen and noticed a small stain on the wall below the cabinets. Life was busy and the spot was hard to see, so I didn't give it much thought. But as time passed, the spot seemed to grow. I'd pass it off as my imagination and go on my way. Then over the next few weeks, there would occasionally be water on the counter. I'd chalk it up as an innocent spill and wipe it clean, never dreaming there could be a connection.

That is, until one morning I noticed the water again. This time it was streaming down the wall and onto the floor! I panicked. The sound of the shower cued me to the water's source, so I yelled at the kids to race upstairs and have their dad turn off the water. With that, the waterfall stopped.

After a visit from the water removal company, we were shocked to discover the real problem. When the builders installed the cabinets, rather than locating studs behind the wall to anchor the cabinets, they used the *drainpipe* from the upstairs bathroom. As a result, they drilled eight large screws through the wall and into the bathroom drainpipe.

This meant every time water flowed from the shower, it leaked through the holes in the drainpipe, soaking the space behind the wall. And the stain on the wall? You guessed it—mold. A small stain from my vantage point but a raging infestation beneath.

What a mess.

Clearly, our problem was more than a wet countertop or stained wall. There was something going on behind the wall we couldn't see. And what we could not see was impacting what we could see.

Have you ever thought the same could be true in our lives? What if there's more going on than we see? What if something we can't see affects what we can see?

Think about your own struggles. Have you ever wondered if the resistance you feel—the discouragement, doubt, depression, division, tension, and temptation—could be sourced by something veiled from your eyes?

That morning in the kitchen, it wasn't until we pulled back the layers that we knew what was happening. We saw the misplaced screws, the perforated pipe, and the mold blanketing the wall's interior. Once we saw behind the wall, we knew how to fix the problem. And the most striking part? What was happening behind the wall—though veiled from our eyes—was just as real as what we could see.

What if it's true that we wrestle not against flesh and blood but against spiritual forces of evil (Eph. 6:12)? What if our weapons are not of this world (2 Cor. 10:4)?

Now, of course, I'm not suggesting every depressing thought, setback, or bad day springs from the forces of darkness. Interestingly, when the prophet Elijah lacked peace to the point of despair, God's solution began with two good meals and a nap (1 Kings 19). Not too shabby.

Still, Scripture is clear regarding an Enemy whose goal is our destruction (1 Peter 5:8). I'm convinced if we pull back the layers and expose what is hidden, we'll be one step closer to not being controlled by his devices.

Today we'll open Scripture and peer behind the wall. We'll expose how the Enemy worked in the beginning and how he works in our lives. Most importantly, we'll uncover Scripture's first promise of Jesus and how he triumphs over every veiled force behind the wall.

What Did God Say?

In the first two chapters of Genesis, we read of the physical world created by God. But a pivot happens in chapter 3, where we encounter another dimension to God's creation—the unseen forces of good and evil and an unseen Enemy.

We begin with the Bible's eye-opening first description of this enemy: "Now the serpent was more crafty than any other beast" (v. 1).

Crafty. This isn't about Mod Podge or glue guns. *Crafty* speaks of someone who cleverly schemes against prey. It describes deception so slight and subtle we may miss or misdiagnose it. We may think it's just a small stain on the wall.

What are Satan's schemes? We see them play out in the garden of Eden. God placed Adam and Eve in a garden of fruit-producing trees, vines, and bushes in a landscape that exceeds our imagination. We don't know how many trees were in the garden, but we do know there was *one* tree from which they should not eat.

Centrally placed, this tree was a constant reminder to Adam and Eve that they were not in charge but were under the loving care of their Creator. The Enemy, however, voiced a different message. He said to the woman, "Did God really say, 'You must not eat from any tree in the garden'?" (v. 1 NIV).

Though this passage may be familiar, notice how Satan twisted God's words. The Serpent asked if God had told them that they could not eat from any of the trees. But that's not what God had said. He said they could *freely* eat from *every* tree, except the Tree of the Knowledge of Good and Evil. God was good and gracious, granting Adam and Eve access to hundreds, if not thousands, of satisfying options. But from the start, Satan portrayed God as controlling and untrustworthy.

The Lie

After twisting God's words, Satan charged with a blatant lie: "You will not surely die" (v. 4). In the most cunning way possible, Satan cast confusion on God's word and concealed sin's consequence of death, saying Eve could do what she pleased. It's as if they could have what they wanted risk free.

Isn't that what we see today? The Enemy whispers lies:

- *You can gossip without hurting others or yourself.*
- *You can tell white lies to make life easier.*
- *You can look at that website or scroll for hours without it affecting you.*

The message is indulge, enjoy, explore. Don't let God control you. Just have fun. It won't affect you. Sound familiar?

Now, lean in and take note. When Satan approached the first couple in the garden, he didn't come with a physical weapon. Instead, he planted a thought in Eve's mind. An idea aimed at casting confusion and poking holes in her flow of thought—a bit of trickling water behind the wall.

And if you and I were to trace the Enemy's actions throughout the pages of Scripture and into our lives, we might be surprised to discover this remains his strategy. He'll place an idea—any idea—in our minds to subtly move us away from God's will.

As I think of the Enemy's schemes, I can't help but remember the evening I was baptized as a little girl. Though the morning had begun with excitement, by afternoon dread and confusion paralyzed my mind. I cried at the kitchen table for hours, telling my mom I didn't have enough faith. Fear tormented me. It was a feeling unlike anything I had experienced, even to this day.

What if I'm not saved? What if I don't have enough faith? The crying did not and would. Not. Stop.

As I think back to that afternoon, I believe the Enemy was at work, launching his fiery darts of condemnation and shame. Through Satan's lies masked as my own thoughts, I questioned the goodness of God and the sufficiency of my faith.

No swords or spears. But ideas, thoughts, and lies.

These tactics are central to how the Enemy works. Therefore, to stand against his schemes, we must tether ourselves to truth—to what God says. Why? Because the battle we fight—the war behind the wall—is a battle over whether we live by what is true or what is a lie.

A Healthy Snack

Let's take a moment and make this practical. If you're like me, you may wonder what's so bad about eating a piece of fruit. Shouldn't the sin that marshaled evil into the world be more substantial? Perhaps a theft, murder, or adultery. But a healthy snack? Really?

The fact that this first sin wasn't an obvious evil helps us understand the true root of Adam and Eve's rebellion: disobedience to God's command. More specifically, Adam and Eve tried to fulfill a good desire apart from God's plan. What do I mean? Eve took the fruit because it was beautiful, delicious, and could make her wise—all good desires. However, the Enemy took these desires and convinced Eve that his path paved the way to fulfillment.

If you and I peer behind the drywall of our sinful struggles, we may find something similar. For example, if we are tempted by alcohol, food, materialism, or lust, perhaps our deeper desires are comfort, control, satisfaction, or peace of mind. Yet we believe the lie that natural things satisfy us, rather than connection to God.

If gossip is our struggle, perhaps the deeper desire is connecting with others or feeling better about ourselves. We believe the lie that gossip is the means to connection and self-worth. Or if we find ourselves chasing beauty, perfection, or achievement, perhaps we believe the lie that our worth, importance, and identity stem from those things rather than a relationship with our Creator.

While these deeper desires are not sinful, when we ignore God's Word to fulfill them, the Enemy has us right where he wants us.

And did you catch the irony? When we ignore God to get more, we're left with less. *Always.* It's a downward spiral that leaves us powerless, depressed, and lacking intimacy with God.

> ## When we ignore God to get more, we're left with less.

Why is it so important we realize this? Because the trajectory of our lives hinges on whether we believe lies or live by God's truth, whether we seek things to satisfy us or know that what he gives is enough.

Hide-and-Seek

When Adam and Eve ate the fruit, sin entered the world. And yet the events that followed carry incredible meaning for them and for us as well. Scripture says that after they ate, "they realized they were naked; so they sewed fig leaves together and made coverings for themselves. . . . and they hid from the LORD God among the trees of the garden" (Gen. 3:7–8 NIV).

Can't you just see Adam and Eve frantically sewing fig leaves, creating their own camouflage of sorts, and scurrying to find the best hiding spot? But God would not let the couple stay in separation, trying to conceal their sin. He called to Adam with a question: "Where are you?" (v. 9).

Of course, God knew where they were. But through these words, God signaled to Adam, Eve, and every heavenly host watching that he would not abandon the man and woman who had rebelled against him.

Adam and Eve hid their presence, but God revealed his.

There would be consequences and curses, yes. But through the question "Where are you?" God expressed his unfailing love. He desired relationship. He wanted them to know their broken responses—running, hiding, and pretending—were not needed.

Can you relate to Adam and Eve's response? Are you ever timid before God because you know your failures? Or do you ever find yourself wanting to camouflage behind the wilting leaves of good works, religion, busyness, or distraction?

It's easy to distance ourselves from God when feeling shame or regret. But the all-seeing, all-loving God who called to Adam and Eve in the garden calls to you and me.

Whatever your situation, don't think that what you've done or what's been done to you keeps you from God's loving arms. If a holy and perfect God could forgive us of the wrong we've done, how much more should we forgive ourselves and walk free from the weight of guilt and shame? Even when we fall to the Enemy's schemes, we don't need to run. We can know God is there, drawing us back to a relationship with him.

How can we know? Because of what we're about to see God do next.

A Covering

In the misery of the moment, Adam and Eve tried to conceal what they couldn't hide. But God was behind the scenes, preparing something for them. "The Lᴏʀᴅ God made garments of skin for Adam and his wife and clothed them" (Gen. 3:21 ɴɪᴠ).

God *himself* made clothes and covered them.

Let's pause and consider how this would have happened. In that lush and beautiful garden among the grazing animals, the holy hand of heaven would have fallen and struck the life of an innocent animal. Through that death, God covered the nakedness of the man and woman and revealed that relationship with him is not based on human efforts. From the opening pages of the Bible, we see God move in breathtaking pictures of redemption.

Isn't this a picture of what Jesus did for you and me?

Thousands of years later, the holy hand of heaven would fall again. But this time it wouldn't strike an innocent animal—it would strike God's innocent Son.

The shedding of blood. Sacrifice. Innocent for the guilty.

And through faith in Jesus, our shame is covered, and we are placed in right standing with God.

The First Gospel
While the garments of skin point to Jesus, nestled in the following passage is a promise that may be less familiar. A promise glistening with hope of the coming Christ. Speaking a curse to the Serpent, God said,

I will cause hostility between you and the woman,
and between your offspring and her offspring.
(Gen. 3:15 ɴʟᴛ)

41

God announced there would be conflict between the serpent and the woman and between their respective offspring. This describes the battle between the seen and unseen world that has continued through the ages.[1] The reality of what's behind the wall.

But God didn't stop there. He continued by revealing what would ultimately happen between these opposing forces. Describing the offspring, God said:

He will strike your head,
and you [Satan] will strike his heel.
(v. 15 NLT)

What was God saying? Though the Enemy successfully deceived Adam and Eve, God would one day strike the head of the Serpent through the woman's descendant. And the descendant? Jesus. The One who would crush the Serpent's head, redeeming us from the curse and bringing ultimate victory over sin and evil. Incredible.

Sin broke our relationship with God in a way we could not fix, yet to the very first couple on the planet, God promised he would restore what was broken. Theologians refer to this promise as the proto-evangelium, meaning the "first gospel."[2]

That's precisely what it is. The first mention of the good news of Jesus. Genesis 3:15 begins a thrilling line of prophecies, promises, and stories that point to the good news of Jesus—prophecies and promises we'll discover through our journey together.

When Our Eyes Are Open

There's one final story I want to show you to bolster your faith and bring today's study together. In 2 Kings, we find God's prophet Elisha surrounded by an enemy army. Elisha's servant saw the massive army and panicked, but Elisha had a different perspective: "Do not be afraid, for those who are with us are more than those who are with them" (6:16).

Was Elisha kidding or was there something the servant could not see—a trickling behind the wall? Elisha asked God to open the servant's eyes, and instantly the servant's perspective changed. He looked and "the mountain was full of horses and chariots of fire all around Elisha" (v. 17). God peeled back the layers, and the servant discerned what had been there all along—an *unseen* army fighting on his behalf!

It's easy to feel overwhelmed by what comes against us, isn't it? Relational conflict, depression, temptation, division, addiction, discouragement, and unexplainable heaviness. But what Elisha's servant realized is what we must remember. Unseen angelic hosts *outnumber* the forces of evil. While we may or may not have chariots of fire surrounding us, John assured us that "he who is in you is greater than he who is in the world" (1 John 4:4). Hallelujah!

Truth and Trust

The afternoon leading up to my baptism ended well but not without a fight. What finally freed me from the unseen battle was Mom pouring love and truth into my heart, reminding me that salvation is nothing we achieve. It's all about receiving the gift God has given. She tethered my racing emotions to God's Word. His truth led me to trust.

Are you sensing areas of resistance or evidence of the Enemy's hand? Are there lies you might identify as coming from the Enemy's arsenal? What if you pull back the layers, expose the Enemy's schemes, and replace his lies with truth? What if you could begin seeing the infinite power of the One who lives in you and me?

Know this: God never intended us to live under the constant weight of confusion, fear, and discouragement. He never intended us to chase after the world's empty idols, always seeking but never satisfied. He desires us to know the fullness of who he is, the liberating power of his truth, and a life of freedom and joy.

It's not an instant fix. It's a lifetime of learning and living by truth and trust. As we journey through the Old Testament and watch God's faithfulness to his people, we'll see truth that can help us rise above lies and live in peace.

How do we not fall to the Enemy's schemes? Where do we begin?

Submit to God.
Cling to truth.
Resist the devil.
Pray without ceasing.
And having done everything, stand.[3]

Because the God who can—and one day will—wipe out Satan is the same God who lives in and empowers you and me.

Questions

Have you ever considered that things we cannot see impact what we can see?

Day 2 | Man's Sin, God's Promise

If you were to identify one specific lie Satan keeps telling you, what would it be?

Think of the lie you just identified. What is God's truth that corresponds to it?

When you are tempted to find satisfaction through other things (shopping, food, achievement, beauty), what are the deeper desires your heart longs for? Ask the Holy Spirit to show you.

How will you start letting God satisfy you in this area?

JESSE TREE
What is something you want to remember about Adam and Eve?

Day 3

NOAH:
WALKING WITH GOD

Read Genesis 6:5–22; 9:8–17; Hebrews 11:7.

I couldn't believe my eyes when I saw it. While driving home from an electric week of camp—worship music blaring and heart praising—I noticed a man walking beside the road, wearing jeans and a black shirt. Between the series of red lights and his pace on foot, we inched side by side through the small town. I didn't think much of it until I glanced at his shirt and gasped in shock. Big, bold yellow letters read, "Say you love Satan."

Day 3 | Noah: Walking with God

Say you love Satan? Is this guy for real?

He disappeared, and I continued home. But no matter how hard I tried, I could not shake the shirt's image from my mind. *Say you love Satan? Say you love Satan?* I repeated to myself in the now quiet car.

After several minutes of debating my options, I could not resist. I made a quick U-turn and raced back to the small town in pursuit of the man in the crazy shirt. To my surprise, the streets were empty. Rather than taking this as my cue to return home, I continued driving until I saw him sitting on a park swing.

I slid out of the car and casually approached him. "Hey! I noticed your shirt . . ."

"What about it?" He shrugged.

I fumbled for words. "I . . . I just don't think it's a good shirt. That's all."

Silence.

Then going straight for the punch, I asked, "Do you know Jesus?" Clearly this was neither a wise decision nor the ideal approach to evangelism. And yet what shocked me more than the message on his shirt was what he said next: "I *do* know Jesus. I'm a Christian. I said a prayer in church when I was a little boy."

My heart sank.

My conversation in the park that afternoon reminds me that a relationship with God is far more than saying a prayer at a service. It's more than attending church or calling ourselves Christian. It's even more than saying we believe in God.

From the beginning, God has desired a relationship with his creation, and he desires a relationship with you.

Catching God's Eye

Yesterday, we ended with the promise of Genesis 3:15—a stunning statement that a Redeemer would come through the woman's seed. Today, only six chapters into Genesis, the forces of evil have saturated society, and the world God created for relationship has turned to rebellion.

Scripture says, "The LORD saw that the wickedness of man was great in the earth, and that *every* intention of the thoughts of his heart was *only* evil *continually*. And the LORD regretted that he had made man on the earth, and it grieved him to his heart" (Gen. 6:5–6).

Do you sense the intensity? *Every* intent was *only* evil. *Continually*.

From the holy perspective of heaven, the world had listened to Satan's lies and ravaged the paradise of God, one rebellious choice at a time. As a result, God grieved and decided to blot out man from the face of the earth (v. 7).

Yet when God scanned the world broken by sin, his eyes danced with delight at the life of one man: "But Noah found favor in the eyes of the LORD. . . . Noah was a righteous man, blameless in his generation. Noah walked with God" (vv. 8–9).

Noah walked with God. Don't you love the simplicity of this statement? Of all the people God could have chosen, he didn't select someone defined by skill, success, salary, or social media status. He didn't choose the one with the most charisma. He didn't choose the one with position or prestige. God's eyes locked on the one who walked with him.

As a result, Noah would be the one through whom God would sovereignly save a remnant of people.

Nothing Too Tricky

After announcing the coming flood, God instructed Noah on the next step. "Make yourself an ark of gopher wood" (v. 14). *Easy enough*, Noah may have thought. I can just see Noah nodding his head in agreement as he listened to God's instructions. Perhaps Noah imagined something comparable to a canoe, pontoon, or oversized raft. Nothing too tricky.

But can you picture Noah's expression as God detailed the ark's dimensions? The ark would stretch 450 feet long, 75 feet wide, and 45 feet tall.[1] In modern terms, it would extend longer than ten school buses end to end and soar more than three stories high.

Imagine what this assignment would entail. In a world before electric drills, circular saws, and YouTube videos, Noah would harvest every tree for this massive vessel.[2] Then, using the most primitive tools, he would meticulously form and seal each beam to withstand the water's fierce force. This was no weekend project or summer job. Noah built the ark over one hundred *years*.

Do you ever wonder how Noah handled this assignment? Did he move forward with confidence? Or did weeks, months, or years pass by when he felt discouraged or wanted to give up? Did his wife and children have much to say? Did he doubt his ability to complete the task?

While we do not know Noah's day-to-day feelings, the book of Hebrews gives us a glimpse into his heart: "By faith Noah, when warned about things not yet seen, in holy fear built an ark to save his family" (11:7 NIV). By faith and in holy fear. Simply put, Noah walked in obedience.

For Noah, *obedience* meant trusting God when it did not make sense. It meant clinging to God's word when people didn't understand or mocked his actions. Obedience was about moving forward, not back. In faith and trust, not fear.

If it were me, I would have panicked, purchased the best equipment possible, and rallied every general contractor in town. I would have concealed my "project" as long as possible for fear of ridicule. Not Noah.

Surrounded only by creation and a mocking world, the simple sound of Noah's obedience—the chopping, pounding, and positioning—filled the air as he crafted the image God deposited into his heart. God's presence, the trees surrounding him, and the faith to believe were all Noah had.

And that would be enough.

Impossible Situations
Is Noah's situation something to which you can relate? Sure, you're not building a boat, but you may be in a situation that feels like an impossibility and the weight of it is stealing your joy. Maybe you're overwhelmed by the responsibility of caring for your children or an aging parent. Perhaps you're a single mom trying to support a family and don't know if you can sustain the pace. Maybe you're leading a ministry, and the demands feel overwhelming. You might be trying to live out your faith at work, but you are ostracized by others and mocked for your beliefs.

Day 3 | Noah: Walking with God

If you're like me, we set out to follow God, and at first his directive seems attainable: work this job, start this business, lead this small group, foster this child, move to this city, serve this person. Yet as we experience the sacrifice of what the task involves, the challenge sets in.

We think, *Should I be doing this? Can this be right? It feels like too much.*

Often we become overwhelmed when we carry the burden ourselves. We trust in our strength rather than God's. Have you been there?

Let this truth encourage your heart: Whatever you're facing, God has not called you to do it alone. He's there and invites you into a partnership of trust and walking with him. And as we walk with him, we see life through a different and liberating lens. Rather than being flooded by our insufficiencies, straining to achieve, and doubting God's sovereignty, we can put our hand in his, knowing Jesus is there, empowering us with his presence and drawing us to a relationship of trust.

What is the task that God has put before you, the one that feels unreachable? The one you know is impossible to complete in your own strength? What if you approach it through the life-infusing lens of walking with God? What if you could wake each day with a sense of partnership with God rather than isolation and defeat? What if you could give yourself grace for your mistakes and focus on his presence with you?

You can raise your children, finish the degree, grow the business, lead the team, teach the class, serve others with love, engage with coworkers, and follow his Spirit, all with the awareness that God is with you.

Despite the uncertainty about the future, what kept Noah moving forward was what qualified him from the start: Noah walked with God.

More to the Story

Noah's ark is a tremendous story. A massive boat, an incredible storm, a stunning rainbow, and an assembly of animals like no other. Its memory plays out in everything from bedding to preschools, amusement parks to animal hospitals. And if we're not careful, we can reduce Noah's ark to a flood and floating parade of animals.

But in the landscape of Scripture, this story is much more. Noah's ark is a picture of God's power, holiness, and glorious plan to save man from sin.

As I studied Noah's ark, here's what I found intriguing. In the chapters devoted to Noah and the flood, we see nothing of what Noah said. *Nothing.* No conversations, dialogue, or inner dialogue.

Though I'm sure he spoke during those hundred years (he was married, after all), the Bible chose not to record it. In fact, we hear nothing from him until after the rain had come and gone.

Perhaps the flood isn't as much about Noah as it is about God: his character, holiness, and plan of salvation. What if it's not as much a showcase of animals as a glimpse into God's sorrow over sin and gracious plan to save? What if it's not only a past event but a picture of something to come?

In the New Testament, Jesus explained, "For as in those days before the flood they were eating and drinking, marrying and giving in marriage, until the day when Noah entered the ark, and they were unaware until the flood came and swept them all away, so will be the coming of the Son of Man" (Matt. 24:38–39).

Don't miss the weight of Jesus's words. Those living in Noah's day were going about their lives, assuming their actions carried no consequence. When the flood came, every person not secured within the walls of the ark perished. With this image in mind, Jesus said, "So will be the coming of the Son of Man."

Jesus identified the flood as a divine foreshadowing of his return. And when Jesus returns, those on the earth will not receive alerts on their phone or warnings from the Emergency Broadcast System. The world will be living its everyday life, and then he will come.

Peter's Warning

Peter also drew a parallel between the flood and Christ's coming. He warned that in the last days scoffers will mock Christians who believe Jesus will return to earth (2 Peter 3:3–4). Peter continued with a chilling warning. Just as the earth was destroyed by water, "the present heavens and earth are reserved for fire, being kept for the day of judgment and destruction of the ungodly" (v. 7 NIV).

Intense, isn't it? It's one we can't casually read between social media scrolls or sips of our favorite latte. Frankly, this verse stops me in my tracks. But as challenging as this verse is to consider, it's important that we understand what it means. To put it simply, Peter said that for the first judgment, God used water. And for the judgment to come, he will use fire.

Though the message is alarming, let me assure you, there is good news.

Truth and Trust

This good news is no better stated than by Jesus himself. The verses may be familiar, but they come alive as we filter them through the lens of today's study. "For God so loved the world, that he gave his only Son, that whoever believes in him should *not perish* but have eternal life. For God did not send his Son into the world to condemn the world, but in order that the world might be *saved* through him" (John 3:16–17).

Do you see the parallels between Noah's day and ours? Just as the ark was Noah's escape from a judgment the world had never known, Jesus is *our* escape from the coming judgment of fire. Jesus is our ark of safety—a guarantee of salvation for the judgment to come. But unlike Noah's ark, our salvation is not produced by our own strength or efforts. Our salvation, our ark of safety, is received by faith.

And there's more. Not only does Noah's ark provide a picture of salvation, it also reveals God's faithfulness to his promise in Genesis 3:15—from Eve's seed, God would bring a Redeemer.

Think of this. If God had destroyed all humanity through the flood, he would have eliminated the lineage through which the Redeemer would come. But staying true to his promise, God spared Noah's family and ultimately the Offspring who would save you and me—Jesus, our salvation and ark of safety.

Was the flood extreme? Yes, but its severity reveals the extent to which God will go to cleanse the earth and establish a relationship with his people. It's second only to the greatest act God did to bring us into a relationship with him—the death of his Son.[3] Hallelujah.

Whatever fears you face, whatever your concern for tomorrow, take joy in your salvation in Christ.

Place your hand in his.
Walk the path together.
Stay faithful to what he has called you to do.
He is with you.

Questions

Can you think of someone who demonstrates a life of walking with God? What makes his or her life unique?

Are you in a situation now that seems like an impossibility? Or is there something you once felt God led you to do that you have put to the side?

What have you learned from Noah's situation that will inspire you to move forward?

How does the idea of a coming judgment affect you?

Do you know two or three people who need to hear the gospel? Share these names with a praying friend and ask God together to soften their hearts.

JESSE TREE

What is something you want to remember about Noah's ark?

TRACING
HIS
Faithfulness
THROUGH
ABRAHAM

Day 4

ABRAHAM:
WHEN GOD PROMISES
THE IMPOSSIBLE

Read Genesis 12:1–3; 15:1–21; Romans 4:19–25.

My husband and I celebrated twenty-three years of marriage this year. Though it may sound odd, one of the things I loved about Ryan from the start was his sense of responsibility. Even as a college freshman, Ryan worked in the school's president's office and as a residential assistant, all while maintaining a sparkly GPA. He lived and breathed productivity and responsibility.

He would confess: to a *fault*.

When Ryan found out he was going to be a dad, his sense of responsibility kicked into high gear, which meant buying a safer vehicle to replace our compact car. But like most young couples, our bank account could not fund the fancy SUVs we envisioned.

Would we take out a loan like the rest of the world? Nope. Not Ryan. Instead, he scoured the internet and found a safe *and* affordable car—an old baby-blue Grand Marquis. I'll add, this was not what I saw myself driving as a young mom.

One week after buying the car, I received a call I'll never forget. A nervous woman's voice muttered, "Hello. Are you Donna?"

"Yes?"

"I've made a terrible mistake!"

"What is it?"

"When you bought my car, I brought the wrong paper to the bank. I brought the title for my mobile home. You own my house!"

We could not believe it!

We dashed to the bank and endured the tedious and time-consuming process of un-purchasing her house, selling her house back, and then buying the car. Purchasing the car the first time was a hassle. Undoing the deal was nuts.

Day 4 | Abraham: When God Promises the Impossible

Why? Because during the original transaction we had signed a contract, what would have been called a *covenant* in Old Testament times. It was a solemn, binding agreement—something not designed to be modified, undone, or terminated.

How does this connect to our study?

Today and throughout our journey together, we'll see God make covenants and promises to his people. Not about houses or cars but covenants revealing his loving provision, care, and plan.

Here's what we'll need to remember. Though Ryan and I reversed the exchange, God's promises are different. They are unshakable and unchanged. Covenants are firmly sealed. Every promise is yes and amen (2 Cor. 1:20).

This is refreshing for us to remember because life can feel so uncertain. The unexpected occurs, plans change, things come and go, and loss happens.

Today you may be unsettled by uncertainty. There may be a situation in your family that's troubling your heart. Perhaps what's happening in the world or your workplace has you feeling uncertain. Or maybe you've received news that has turned your life upside down.

So often it's the unknown that troubles us, isn't it? But through our journey together, we'll realize God holds *all* things together. We'll see that Jesus's coming to earth wasn't something God spontaneously decided in response to a broken world. Rather, Christ existed *before the world* and was *chosen before* the world (Col. 1:17; 1 Peter 1:20). What a thought!

Today we'll watch God's plan unfold as he makes a covenant that is the basis and foundation for all the covenants that follow—the Abrahamic covenant.[1] And the best part? We'll discover how God fulfilled this promise through Jesus. And as we see God's faithfulness to fulfill these and other promises, we'll be assured of his faithfulness and continual care for you and me.

The Seed of Salvation

In Genesis 12, God spoke to Abraham and said, "Go from your country . . . to the land that I will show you. And I will make of you a great nation, and I will bless you and make your name great, so that you will be a blessing. . . . In you all the families of the earth shall be blessed" (vv. 1–3).

God promised Abraham land, blessing, and offspring. But there was a problem (and a big one). Abraham was seventy-five years old and childless. He and his lovely yet aging wife, Sarah, had experienced a lifetime of infertility. But God, as he so beautifully does, made a promise and would accomplish the impossible.

When we think of Abraham's offspring, we may think of his son Isaac and the descendants who followed. But in the New Testament, we learn there's *another* promise nestled in God's words to Abraham. It's a promise that makes my heart leap with excitement. It's about *who* Abraham's offspring—his seed—would be.

The apostle Paul told us the "promises were spoken to Abraham and to his seed. Scripture does not say 'and to seeds,' meaning many people, but 'and to your seed,' meaning one person, who is Christ" (Gal. 3:16 NIV).

Do you see what Paul was saying? Though Abraham had Isaac and countless descendants, God's promise to Abraham spoke of *one* offspring, or one "seed." Paul was letting us know the *ultimate* blessing would come through one man—Jesus.[2]

Day 4 | Abraham: When God Promises the Impossible

It's the promise of Jesus in Genesis!

As we journey through the Old Testament, we'll discover that the stories that follow are not mere history lessons. Rather, we'll trace a storyline that culminates with the person of Jesus himself.[3]

This promise to Abraham was such a peak and pinnacle moment that the New Testament opens by peering back to this promise. The gospel of Matthew begins, "The book of the genealogy of Jesus Christ, the son of David, the *son of Abraham*" (1:1).

And there's more. When God originally spoke to Abraham, he said, "In you all the families of the earth shall be blessed" (Gen. 12:3). How could *all* families be blessed through Abraham? Because through Abraham the Messiah would come! The One who would offer the best blessing imaginable: salvation to the entire world (Gal. 3:7–9).

Are you seeing the unity and brilliance of Scripture? The promise of a coming Redeemer whispered to Adam and Eve in the garden is shouted through God's promise to Abraham.

A Redeemer would come to bless the world!

Fully Convinced

Before we go further, I want to pause and let Abraham's faith encourage our hearts. For Abraham, the question was clear: Would he believe what he could see or what God said?

It's a question we face as well. Will we hold to feeling or fact, what we see or what God says? If you're like me, you want to believe, but as time passes weariness sets in. Doubt becomes familiar. We wonder, *Will things change? Will God answer my cry?*

The other morning, I awoke with similar questions. I'd pray, then doubt. Worship, then worry. Then in the quietness of my room, I remembered Abraham and a verse describing his faith. Paul said Abraham "did *not* weaken in faith when he considered his own body, . . . or when he considered the barrenness of Sarah's womb" (Rom. 4:19).

I love that Abraham didn't ignore his limitations or live in denial. He didn't pretend everything was perfect and then scroll his phone to pass the time. Scripture says he *"considered* his own body." Abraham didn't stop there: "He grew strong in his faith as he *gave glory to God*, fully convinced that God was able to do what he had promised" (vv. 20–21).

Abraham's faith flourished as he gave glory to God—as he *worshiped*.

Once I spotted this detail, I knew this was the Spirit's whisper to me that morning. God wasn't calling me to rehearse my frustrations or to waver in worry and self-pity. Instead, he was calling me to follow Abraham's example of trust and worship.

This is the kind of faith we desire, isn't it? Let Abraham's faith-filled response encourage your heart. He worshiped rather than worried. He trusted God even in the delay, even when God's plan didn't make sense.

And as we will see next, Abraham's belief moved him to an extraordinary blessing.

The Gospel in Genesis

Ten years passed for Abraham, and what may have seemed like an impossibility at seventy-five would be a mind-boggling miracle at eighty-five. Still, time never weakens God's promise.

Day 4 | Abraham: When God Promises the Impossible

God spoke to Abraham again: "Look toward heaven, and number the stars, if you are able to number them. . . . So shall your offspring be" (Gen. 15:5). It's as if God was saying, "Abraham, don't look at the problem. Believe my promise. Trust what I say."

Time never weakens God's promise.

In response to God's promise, Abraham "believed the LORD, and he counted it to him as righteousness" (v. 6).

Here lies the profound exchange that sets the salvation story in motion. Abraham *believed*, and God declared him righteous. It wasn't about the works Abraham did or did not do. It was about his faith. And the best part? Just as Abraham believed and God counted him righteous, when you and I believe in the Offspring—Jesus—God counts us righteous! It's a past event that points to a present reality.

It's the blueprint for our salvation—salvation through faith.

The apostle Paul peered back at this moment in Abraham's life and made a brilliant connection: "When God counted him [Abraham] as righteous, it wasn't just for Abraham's benefit. It was recorded for *our* benefit, too, assuring us that God will also count us as righteous if we believe in him" (Rom. 4:23–24 NLT).

Don't miss what Paul is saying. When God counted Abraham righteous, it wasn't unique to Abraham. It was "for our benefit, too." Paul is telling us that salvation by faith is available for all who believe. Then and now.

It's the gospel—in Genesis.

One Woman's Heart

Being in a right relationship with God isn't about our efforts, works, or living a good life. It's a gift of grace, not works (Eph. 2:8–9). This is important to remember because in a world where the gospel is often confused, it's easy to hold false conclusions about salvation.

This was the case with Mandi, a woman who attended a Bible study I was leading. Mandi appeared to have it all together. She was energetic, attractive, and active in the community. But despite her outward success, Mandi struggled with performance-based acceptance. She had a hard time receiving God's love and had always been taught that good works merited salvation.

The night before one of our studies, I was looking for an illustration to review what salvation means. Passing through my bedroom, I saw an unopened package of white T-shirts on the bed and had my answer.

I rushed into my husband's closet, grabbed an old T-shirt, and headed outside to drag it through the mud. (I didn't think he'd mind.) Once inside, I pulled a gleaming white shirt from the package and tossed both shirts into my bag.

The next morning at Bible study, I held up the stained shirt, explaining that we are stained and sinful without God. Then I displayed the clean white shirt. I explained that when we place our faith in Jesus, God forgives our sins, and with forgiveness comes the gift of snow-white righteousness and eternal life.

While sharing what I assumed was a review, I sensed someone was understanding God's gift of salvation for the first time. I stopped and asked if anyone wanted to confess faith in Jesus and receive the gift of righteousness. At a table in the back of the room, Mandi slipped up her hand. What a morning!

The blessing of God's promise—the Seed in whom *all* the nations would be blessed—extended to *one* woman's heart who believed. And God, as he did with Abraham, counted Mandi righteous and gave her eternal life—not because of her works but because of her faith in him.

The Supernatural Display

Abraham believed and God declared him righteous. But God wasn't finished revealing his power. One final and fascinating detail brings today's lesson together: "On that day the LORD made a covenant with Abram" (Gen. 15:18).

A covenant. When you or I make a covenant, we sign an agreement on paper. It's when we take out a loan or exchange vows in marriage. Or when we buy a car or house—or in our case, a house instead of a car.

But in ancient culture, covenants often involved animal sacrifice. If that wasn't odd enough, to formalize the covenant both parties would position carcasses on the ground and walk between the pieces of bloody flesh, signifying the gravity of their commitment to each other.[4]

I'll connect this to Abraham. When God made his promise to Abraham, he made a covenant. And as part of the covenant-making ceremony, God told Abraham to take animals and divide their flesh in two. Easy to read, but this involved gathering and killing the animals, then cutting them in half and positioning the carcasses.

Normally, at this point both parties would walk through the pieces of flesh. But you'll love what God does next: "When the sun had set and darkness had fallen, a smoking firepot with a blazing torch appeared and passed between the pieces [of flesh]" (Gen. 15:17 NIV). Imagine the sight. In the dark night, a manifestation of God's presence appeared and literally passed through the pieces of animal flesh.[5]

Here's what makes this even more interesting. Abraham never walked through the pieces of flesh—he was in a deep sleep.

God passed through the pieces. *Alone.*

By walking through the pieces alone, God was confirming his commitment to the promise, regardless of Abraham's actions. And for you and me, God invites us to a covenant not based on our works but on his.

It's salvation by grace through faith in the Offspring—Jesus.

Truth and Trust

We've laid such a rich foundation. I love today's lesson because it provides a deep understanding of our salvation and reminds us of God's faithfulness to his promise. Then and now.

Day 4 | Abraham: When God Promises the Impossible

Consider this. God—in his foreknowledge and supreme sovereignty—knew the Messiah would come through Abraham. Even though Jesus would not come to earth for another two thousand years, God was holding all things together. In his sovereignty, eternal nature, and perfect knowledge, God could say with confidence to Abraham, "From you, the Messiah will come."

Not only that, salvation would be nothing of Abraham's work and all a gift of God's grace. Most of all, just as God invited Abraham into a relationship of faith and trust, God extends the same invitation to you and me. He holds all our todays and tomorrows.

As we continue our journey through the Old Testament, we'll see story after story point back to the precise moment when God made the covenant with Abraham. And the best part? Because Jesus—the Seed—*has* come, we have a front-row seat in watching how these stories speak of him.

What a Savior!

Questions

Abraham waited and worshiped. What is a situation in your life where you could wait and worship rather than worry?

Do you find yourself trying to work for God's love and acceptance? How can today's lesson help you with that?

How does seeing how God orchestrated Christ's coming and our salvation from the beginning help you with the uncertain situations in your life now?

JESSE TREE
What is something you want to remember about Abraham's call and the Seed?

Day 5

ISAAC: DO YOU TRUST ME?

Read Genesis 22:1–18.

"Mom, don't worry. I'm a Christian. I did the right thing."

These were the words from my son when he came home from sports camp last week. Apparently a group of boys chose him as their week-long target of insults and mockery. For a teenage boy with endless energy and a strong sense of justice, it took Isaiah everything he had not to give some ol' fashion retaliation. He was lit up, and I couldn't blame him.

And yet, every time Isaiah shared another story, I had to smile. He'd get worked up and then end by taking a deep breath and saying, "Mom, it was *hard*. But I did the right thing."

This may seem like a simple story, but what Isaiah felt at camp is what we often face in life: the decision to trust and obey God when tested. And whether we realize it or not, it's something we face daily. It's the decision to make the godly choice, flee temptation, givé, forgive, trust, or simply obey God's command.

For my son, knowing *who* he was and *whose* he was made him trust God and do the right thing. But in times of testing we can become so buried by burdens we forget who we are. Not only that, we forget *whose* we are and the promises he's given. We can drift from dependence on God to old patterns of self-reliance and sin. We're tempted to numb the pain, give in to our flesh, and forget the refuge God provides.

But today we'll be encouraged by watching Abraham walk through what was likely the hardest challenge of his life. We'll witness not only a brilliant picture of Christ, but we'll see how Abraham's obedience and trust propelled him to a place of blessing and knowing God more.

A place of confidence, trust, and intimacy we can know as well.

When God Doesn't Make Sense

In yesterday's study, God's promise to Abraham was encouraging and uplifting: blessing, offspring, and land—sunshine on a spring day.

Today is different. God told Abraham to do something that would challenge everything he believed about trusting God: "Take your son, your only son Isaac, whom you love, and go to the land of Moriah, and offer him there as a burnt offering" (Gen. 22:2).

Imagine the shock. For over thirteen years, Abraham had loved and raised Isaac—the very personification of God's faithfulness and the fulfillment of his promise. The one Abraham and Sarah had cradled in their arms, knowing he was a miracle from God.

But God said, "Sacrifice him. Give him to me."

It was a test. Abraham loved Isaac, but did he love God more? Would he obey and trust what God asked him to do?

Here's what made Abraham's situation even more perplexing: God's command seemed to contradict God's plan. In the Abrahamic covenant, God promised Abraham that the Messiah would come through his family. Later in Genesis, God said Isaac is the one through whom the promise would continue (17:21).

Do you sense the tension? How could Abraham sacrifice Isaac when the Messiah would come through Isaac's family? Isaac wasn't married. He didn't have children. It didn't make sense.

And yet Abraham's job wasn't to understand. It was to obey.

No Delay or Hesitation

After receiving God's instruction, "Abraham rose early in the morning, saddled his donkey, and took two of his young men with him, and his son Isaac" (22:3). God spoke. Abraham went. No delay, hesitation, or negotiation.

Does this impress you like it does me? If it were me, I would have stalled until I thought God had changed his mind. If that didn't work, I may have asked some friends if they thought a burnt offering was the best decision for my child's future.

> ### God spoke. Abraham went. No delay, hesitation, or negotiation.

Not Abraham.

He put obedience over understanding—faith over feeling. Whatever Abraham feared did not stop him from moving forward in faith.

Do you ever feel like you're in a similar place? You feel God asking you to trust him in an area of your life or nudging you to release something to his control. A relationship. Your future. Your family. A ministry or dream. Or he may be leading you in a direction that doesn't make sense.

For Abraham, faith wasn't only about believing God for a blessing. It was about trusting God when that blessing might be taken away. It was about surrendering to God and trusting him through the process. It was about believing what God had promised, even when everything said otherwise.

We see this kind of faith in Abraham when he spoke to his servants: "Stay here with the donkey while I and the boy go over there. We will worship and then we will come back to you" (v. 5 NIV).

Don't miss this. *We* will come back—Abraham *and* Isaac. What a statement of faith.

74

Day 5 | Isaac: Do You Trust Me?

If you're like me, reading Abraham's words may make you wonder what he was thinking. Interestingly, Genesis 22 says nothing about Abraham's thoughts. However, the book of Hebrews provides insight: Abraham "considered that God was able even to raise him [Isaac] from the dead" (11:19).

As far as we know, Abraham had never seen someone come back to life. But he reasoned that God could do the impossible. If Isaac was the son through whom the promise would come—which God said he was—then Abraham believed that not even death could stop that from happening.

Isaac's Question

We've looked at Abraham, but we can't forget Isaac, who I'm sure had questions of his own. As they neared the place of sacrifice, Isaac asked, "Behold, the fire and the wood, but where is the lamb for a burnt offering?" (Gen. 22:7).

Picture the scene. Isaac was watching his father prepare the sacrifice, as he had done countless times. But this time Isaac noticed something was different. Something was missing. Perhaps Isaac thought that Abraham, in his old age, had forgotten to bring the sacrifice. Bewildered, Isaac looked at his father and asked, "Where is the lamb?"

Perhaps this was the question Abraham feared most. Apparently Abraham had stayed silent about the sacrifice during their three days of travel through the desert. But now he had to answer Isaac's heart-wrenching question.

Abraham replied, "God himself will provide the lamb" (v. 8 NIV). God *will* provide. Abraham didn't know how the provision would come, but he knew his God and what he had promised.

I think it's easy to define *faith* as simply believing in something we can't see. For example, we might say we believe God exists or we believe in heaven. And while this is certainly part of faith, I see something more. Hebrews describes faith as *confidence* in something we hope for. It is the *assurance* of things we can't see (11:1).

Faith involves having confidence, even when challenged by the unknown, the questions, and the impossibilities. It's a place where what we see or feel may go against what God has spoken. It's where God's goodness and provision can be a perplexing mystery.

And yet, with faith there is an assurance of God's goodness, care, and love. Faith doesn't ignore the questions. Rather, faith says, "God, you are good. I trust in you." In the words of Abraham, faith says, "God himself will provide." It says, "We will go . . . and we will also come back."

> With faith there is an assurance of God's goodness, care, and love.

Do you long for this kind of faith like I do? Perhaps you're in a place of testing that's challenging everything you believe about God's goodness. You want to believe, but the road is long, and you're weary. You have more questions than answers.

How do we respond in those moments? Despite the questions and uncertainty, we continue walking one day at a time, one decision at a time, clinging in dependency and confidence to God's goodness and what he has promised.

Day 5 | Isaac: Do You Trust Me?

God Will Provide

Once Abraham and Isaac were on Mount Moriah, the moment of sacrifice had come. Scripture says Abraham built an altar, "bound his son Isaac and laid him on the altar, on top of the wood. Then he reached out his hand and took the knife to slay his son" (Gen. 22:9–10 NIV).

I can just see Abraham's brow beaded with sweat and tears streaming down his face. He knew God would provide, but where was the provision? Where was God now?

Just as Abraham was about to commit the unthinkable, the miracle occurred. The angel of the Lord called to Abraham and said, "'Do not lay your hand on the boy or do anything to him.' . . . Abraham lifted up his eyes and looked, and behold, behind him was a ram, caught in a thicket by his horns" (vv. 12–13).

Imagine the sweeping relief that rushed through Abraham's body (and Isaac's) when he heard the angel's voice and saw the ram caught in the thicket. Isaac would not be the sacrifice. God had provided the ram in his place.

The promised Redeemer of Genesis 3:15 lives! The promise of God continues. Through the seed of Abraham and now Isaac, all the people of the world would be blessed.

Hallelujah!

Jesus in It All

When my son was younger, I told him the story of Abraham sacrificing Isaac. In his curiosity, he asked me a question I'll never forget: "Mom, what would you do if God told you to sacrifice *me*?"

My heart sank as I considered where his imagination had gone. Yet the answer to his question poignantly captures the heart of this story. I responded, "Don't worry, Isaiah. God wouldn't ask me to sacrifice you. He sacrificed his Son in your place."

Not only is today's story a tremendous demonstration of Abraham's faith, it's also a brilliant picture of Jesus. Consider this:

- Abraham sacrificed his only son, as God did his only Son.
- Isaac and Jesus had supernatural births. Isaac was born to a woman in her nineties, and Jesus was born of a virgin.
- Isaac went willingly to the altar, and Jesus went willingly to the cross.
- Isaac carried the wood, just as Jesus carried his cross.
- Isaac's substitute was the ram in the thicket—a picture of Jesus, not caught in a thicket but wearing a crown of thorns.

Abraham sacrificing his son Isaac is a picture of what would happen two thousand years later between God and his only Son. However, there is one difference. Jesus did not have a substitute. He was *our* substitute. The One God sacrificed in our place. That's why John would later say regarding Jesus, "Behold, the Lamb of God, who takes away the sin of the world!" (John 1:29).

What a Savior!

Truth and Trust

Abraham's story provides an example of faith from which we learn countless lessons. If I could condense today's study down to one simple truth we can hold close to our hearts, it would be this: God's word can be trusted.

God spoke to Abraham, telling him Isaac was the one through whom the promise would continue. Even when everything around Abraham said differently, he believed, knowing that not even death could thwart God's plan.

What I love about Abraham's faith is that it wasn't based on wishful thinking. It wasn't something he crafted in his mind or hoped would come true. Rather, Abraham's faith was secured by God's promise. And when Abraham's situation seemed to counter what God had promised, Abraham clung to what he knew was true.

Could this be an example for us? You may be in a situation that makes you wonder if God is there or if he hears. You may be wondering why things didn't turn out as you hoped or why life feels so challenging. Or perhaps you sense God asking you to trust him or to release something to his hands.

Though our struggles differ from Abraham's (thank you, Jesus), we have opportunities to trust God's word every day. Like Abraham we can walk in surrendered obedience and confident trust. It's an emptying of ourselves and our ability that leads to dependency. And this dependency leads to intimacy.

As we end today's study, I want to give you three promises from the Bible. Three simple truths I use to strengthen my faith and settle my soul when my heart wants to fear. God says:

"I am with you."

"I hear you."

"I work all things for good."

I am with you. Even when we feel alone or our situation says otherwise,

79

even when we're tempted to carry the burden in our own strength, we can trust God is with us (Ps. 46:1).

I hear you. We can trust that when we pray, God hears. When we gaze into the night sky or take long drives in the car to pour out our hearts, God hears every word (Ps. 145:19).

I work all things for good. I'm refreshed by the word *all.* Not some things or a few or most things. All. In his perfect wisdom and love, God works all things together for good for those who love him and are called according to his purpose (Rom. 8:28). He is a redeeming and good God.

Today—in your life and mine—we can stand on these and other promises in the Bible. And when hard times come, we can cling to God in obedience and trust. Dependency and intimacy.

One step at a time.
One day at a time.
One moment at a time.
Because he is faithful to his promise.

Questions

Of the three promises we covered, which one speaks to you the most?

☐ God is with me.
☐ God hears me.
☐ God will work all things for good.

How would you describe Abraham's obedience?

Recall a time when your faith was tested. How did you respond?

How is God speaking to you or encouraging you through the story of Abraham's faith?

JESSE TREE

What is something you want to remember about Abraham's test?

Day 6

JACOB:
YOU'RE NEVER ALONE

Read Genesis 28:10–19.

We're a family who has moved around. A lot. By the time our daughter was in fourth grade, she had attended five different elementary schools. And in only nine months, we lived in four different homes.

I'll add these moves weren't quick skips across town. They were abrupt cross-country moves in which we rented or purchased a home at every stop—exhausting, emotional, and expensive.

When I called the rental company for our most recent move, they replied, "Oh! Mrs. Amidon, it looks like you have used us quite a bit. Tell you what—we'll give you five hundred dollars off this rental. Best of luck!"

I'm pretty sure that doesn't happen every day.

Of all the transitions, the first was the most challenging, because we stopped attending the only church my children had known. When we left the church on our last Sunday, Charity threw herself against the wall muraled with Bible stories she'd grown to love. With all the strength her nine-year-old frame could muster, she gripped the walls, locked her feet to the floor, and cried, "Mom, I don't care what happens. I am *not* leaving."

Not only did my kids question the future and long for familiarity, their hearts needed hope. So did mine.

I don't know the details of your story, but I know when we're pulled from places of comfort and land where we didn't expect, our hearts can become worn. Our minds scatter, and our sense of direction derails. Our relationships strain, tensions build, and we're left with countless questions.

Usually these situations don't involve moving trucks and cardboard boxes. They involve a stripping of the familiar—the things and people we love and find comfort in. We may look back and rehearse how we got to where we are and wish it were a dream. We may replay scenarios and think how things would have been different if we had only, or if they had only. We wonder, *God, are you there? Do you still have a plan for me?*

Jacob may have asked these questions too.

Yesterday we felt the weight of Abraham's surrender and the relief of God's provision. Today we look at Abraham's grandson, Jacob, and how God settled the questions of his heart.

And how he will settle yours.

Escape to Haran

Our story begins with this statement: "Jacob left Beersheba and went toward Haran" (Gen. 28:10). Behind this verse is quite the drama. Jacob's journey was not a retreat or overnight camping trip with the boys. He was running for his life because he had tricked his brother, Esau, into giving him his birthright and blessing.

I suspect this wasn't the first skirmish between the spirited brothers. Even in the womb, Jacob and Esau struggled to the point of their mom asking God for an explanation. This conflict continued to the delivery room table, with Jacob grasping Esau's heel. Fast-forward several years, and the twins grew into their unique selves: Esau, a hunter favored by his dad, and Jacob, his mama's favorite—a modern-day homebody.

One day Esau arrived home from hunting—*hangry*. Jacob, longing to capitalize on his brother's ravenous state, moved in for the deal: "If you give me your birthright, I'll give you my soup." Esau, preferring physical satisfaction over spiritual blessing, agreed to the exchange. His birthright slipped through his fingers as he sipped his brother's soup (25:29–34).

Then there was Jacob's deception against his father, Isaac. Disguising himself as Esau, Jacob tricked Isaac into giving him Esau's blessing. And as you can imagine, an enraged Esau sought to kill his brother (27:1–41).

Hence, Jacob's escape to Haran. Talk about a mess.

A Stunning Sight

Have you ever stopped to consider the experiences and emotions of men and women in the Bible? I remind myself that they weren't super saints with capes and magic daggers. They were real people with real emotions—neither immune to the sting of rejection nor the gnawing of regret and guilt.

I imagine that Jacob felt as we do in seasons of uncertainty: full of fear, regret, anger, and loneliness. He may have even harbored bitterness toward his mother, who had initiated part of the deception. Like my daughter grasping the halls in the church, Jacob likely longed for comfort and the familiar. The irony is that he was running *away* from his family—the very people through whom the stolen birthright would come.

On the run, Jacob slept outside using a rock for a pillow. Yet he had no idea how God would reveal himself. Jacob dreamed, and behold, "there was a ladder set up on the earth, and the top of it reached to heaven. And behold, the angels of God were ascending and descending on it! And behold, the LORD stood above it" (28:12–13).

Pause for a moment and envision the scene. A massive ladder extending to heaven, with angels ascending and descending it. These angels weren't running the stairs like kids on an escalator. They were ministering spirits—ascending to God from earth and descending with heavenly provision.[1]

At the top of the ladder was God himself.

Notice the unique way the author used the word *behold*. "Behold, there was a ladder . . . Behold, the angels . . . Behold, the Lord." It's as if the author leans in, lowers his voice, and whispers, "Come close. Don't miss the beauty of what God did for Jacob through this stunning sight."

What did this all mean? This ladder was the divine connection of God's promises to Jacob's life. It confronted any belief in Jacob that God had forsaken him. More than that, it deposited what he desperately needed—hope.

God was working—even when Jacob was running—and would not let him go. What's more, God delivered a message directly to Jacob: "I am the LORD, the God of Abraham your father and the God of Isaac. . . . And in you and your offspring shall all the families of the earth be blessed. Behold, I am with you and will keep you wherever you go" (vv. 13–15).

These words may sound familiar. This was the same promise God had spoken to Abraham—a promise of land, blessing, and offspring (day 4). Here we see the covenant extends from Abraham to Isaac *and* to Jacob. The Messiah would come through Jacob's lineage!

I find this fascinating. To a man marked by manipulation and deceit, God said, "Through you, I will fulfill my promise." Remember, when God made his covenant with Abraham, he *alone* passed between the pieces of flesh, signifying that the covenant was not based on works but on grace.

And to Jacob, God extended that same grace. Jacob received the promise, not because of his goodness but because of God's faithfulness to his promise.

God with Us

When the kids and I drove away from church on that final Sunday, I knew it would not be easy. My sense of loss coupled with their hurt

Day 6 | Jacob: You're Never Alone

was a crashing wave I couldn't withstand. I whispered a quick prayer, asking God for a way to calm myself and comfort the kids. After several minutes, the words slowly came. I told the kids that though we were leaving a special place, God would be with us in the new place, just as he had always been.

While I comforted my children, something unexpected happened. I listened to my own words, and for the first time in months, faith stirred in my heart. The dark cloud of despair vaporized. I knew I was not alone.

It was the same promise God spoke to Jacob from the ladder. "I am with you and will keep you wherever you go" (Gen. 28:15).

Today, whatever you're facing, know that even when you feel like God isn't there or you're on your own—far from the blessing of God— God's promise to Jacob echoes to you and me: I am with you (Matt. 28:20; Heb. 13:5).

Don't think that where you are right now—sitting in the regret of bad decisions, displaced by the wrong of others, or flailing in an unfamiliar place—has severed the connection between you and the embrace of your loving Father in heaven.

He is there and can settle the questions of your heart.

Jacob's Discovery

When Jacob woke from his vision, he uttered a raw and beautiful re-action: "Surely the LORD is in this place, and I did not know it" (Gen. 28:16). I love this. Through the vision, God gave Jacob a glimpse of what had been there all along—God's presence and activity in his life.

From Jacob's reaction, we can guess this experience countered the lies and fears that may have consumed his mind.

87

Through the vision,

- Jacob realized the nearness of God rather than distance;
- he heard the promise of God rather than his mistakes; and
- he witnessed the activity of heaven rather than feeling abandoned by God.

He didn't have to run or hide. God was there!

There's more. When we step into the New Testament pages, we discover that Jacob's vision carries even greater significance. Early in Jesus's ministry, he revealed himself to Nathanael and used the image of Jacob's ladder to describe his life and ministry: "Truly, truly, I say to you, you will see heaven opened, and the angels of God ascending and descending on the Son of Man" (John 1:51).

Here, the angels are ascending and descending not on a physical ladder but on the Son of Man—Jesus! Through Jesus's explanation to Nathanael, we learn that Jacob's ladder was not just an experience in his life; it pointed to a person—a picture of Jesus Christ who was to come.

Think of what a ladder does. It reaches places we cannot go. It takes us to heights impossible in our own strength. In the same way, Jesus is a ladder.

The New Testament describes how

- he is the connection between God and man (1 Tim. 2:5);
- he is the One interceding for us (Rom. 8:34);
- he is the One through whom we are reconciled to God (2 Cor. 5:18); and
- he is the only way to God (John 14:6; Acts 4:12).

Truth and Trust

I still remember the surge of faith that I experienced on the car ride home that final Sunday. It was a wave of relief and hope. I felt a little like Jacob. God was with us, and I didn't even know it. Nothing had changed externally. But what had changed was my understanding of who had been there the entire time—God and his loving activity in my life.

Could the truth of God's promise and Jacob's response settle the restlessness and weariness in your heart? How would your situation feel different if you remembered Jesus's presence is with you?

Jacob did not deserve the heavenly perspective he gained that night any more than we deserve the blessing of Jesus. Jacob was a man of countless mistakes, as we are. And yet as sinful and conniving as Jacob had been, God's faithfulness and patience were greater still. Jacob's mistakes had not broken the connecting ladder from God's promises to Jacob's life. The ladder was a picture of God's grace, as is Jesus.

> **As sinful and conniving as Jacob had been, God's faithfulness and patience were greater still.**

Let your heart find comfort in his promise today. Though veiled to our natural eyes, Jesus is with you, even when you do not know it. He sees your story and has heard every cry of your heart.

He is working on your behalf.
Your story is not over.
You can have hope.
Rest in that today.

Questions

When you are overwhelmed by life, where do you go to remind yourself of God's presence? Nature? A specific place in your home?

Recall a challenging season from the past or one you are currently facing. Did or does God seem distant or near?

In a situation that concerns you—a rebellious child, struggling marriage, challenges with health—how are you seeing the activity of God?

Jacob said God was with him, even when Jacob did not know it (Gen. 28:16). How would your situation feel different if you remembered God is with you?

JESSE TREE
What is something you want to remember about Jacob's ladder?

Day 7

JOSEPH:
GOD MEANT IT FOR GOOD

Read Genesis 37:3–28; 45:1–8; 50:20.

My daughter received her first pair of glasses in the third grade. Since I also had glasses at a young age, I could not wait to watch Charity's eyes illuminate with wonder as she experienced the world in a new way.

We walked into the doctor's office and Charity plopped on the chair. Within seconds, the eye doctor entered with Charity's new pair of leopard-print glasses. After making a few adjustments, the doctor stepped back so Charity could look around the room. Her eyes bounced from object to object, dancing in delight at the beautiful and crisp new world.

Then she saw me.

Like the flip of a switch, the light in her eyes went dark. She furrowed her brow. Then, in the way only a polite eight-year-old girl could convey, Charity said, "Mom, I like you better *without* my glasses!"

I blurted a quick chuckle to mask the utter humiliation of the moment. Then, I glanced at the eye doctor, who was doing everything possible to refrain from erupting in laughter and doubling over in her swivel chair.

It was a moment to remember.

I love this story because it makes me laugh to this day. I also love it for the reminder it brings: the lens through which we look changes our perspective. Whether in sunglasses or leopard-print glasses, lenses change how we see.

And what is true with our physical eyes is also true with how we perceive situations around us. We may not have glasses, but we have lenses that shape our view of the world. And that lens determines our response to life. For example, when we face setbacks, betrayal, or disappointment, we can view the situation through the lens of worry and fear, questioning God's love and care. Or we can look through the lens of trust and hope, clinging to God in faith and surrendering to his plan.

I don't know about you, but I long to live with a lens of faith and trust in God. I want to view the mountains that look insurmountable and see the faith-filled potential. I want to respond to situations in a way that clings to what God says rather than what I see.

When I consider Scripture and think of someone who lived with that same lens, I think of Joseph. Despite years of betrayal, loss, false accusation, and setbacks, Joseph had a rock-solid faith in God.

Today, we'll watch Joseph live with unwavering faith and trust. Through his story, we will see the bigger story of Jesus advancing. And along the way, by God's grace, we'll know the lens through which our loving Father would have us look.

Favored Son, Hated Brother

Yesterday we saw a stunning image of God's presence in Jacob's life. God was there even though Jacob did not know it. Through God's revelation to Jacob, we learned that the Messiah would come through Jacob's line.

After these events in Genesis, Jacob (renamed Israel) married and had twelve sons who would be known as the twelve tribes of Israel. (There were four wives and a few grandkids in there, but we'll keep it simple.)

Of all his children, Jacob loved Joseph the most.

This love compelled Jacob to give Joseph a gift that sets today's story in motion. "Now Israel [Jacob] loved Joseph *more than* any other of his sons, because he was the son of his old age. And he made him a robe of many colors" (Gen. 37:3).

This robe was more than a luxurious gift or fashion statement. It indicated Jacob's plan to give Joseph authority over his brothers, an honor typically reserved for the oldest child.

Here's where it gets sticky: Joseph was not the oldest. Not even close. He was *eleventh* in the line of burly brothers. And if that didn't frustrate Joseph's brothers enough, there's more.

Day 7 | Joseph: God Meant It for Good

After receiving the coat, Joseph had dreams affirming what the coat symbolized—his ultimate rule over the family. But Joseph, rather than keeping his excitement to himself, broadcast the news to his brothers.

Let's just say that did not go well.

Joseph's brothers had had enough. They stripped Joseph of his coat, threw him in a pit, faked his death, and sold him to traders.

The story may be familiar, but imagine the agonizing rejection in Joseph's heart. Robbed, betrayed, abused, exploited. Separated from family and rejected by not one or two but ten older brothers.

A Redeeming Chapter

As I read Joseph's story, I can't help but recall pain I've experienced. Even more, I think of the women I have counseled who have faced rejection's sting. I've wept with them over their stories of betrayal and hurt. Sometimes pain results from our wrongdoing. Sometimes it results from others' actions. Most often it's a mixture of both. Still, the pain persists.

Can you relate to Joseph's situation? Have you experienced pain or disappointment that made you wonder if life would ever feel normal again? Sometimes it comes at once: unexpected job loss, a rebellious child, an unfaithful spouse, betrayal from a friend, or the loss of a loved one. Sometimes it spans several years: a severed relationship, a sick child, an abusive parent, or a spouse struggling with addiction.

For Joseph, the broken relationship with his brothers was only the beginning. Their betrayal initiated a forced relocation to an unfamiliar country, where Joseph worked in the lowliest of positions—a slave. And for us, broken relationships and betrayal can lead to setback and loss as well.

But there is good news. Despite Joseph's dark situation and disappointment, God was scripting a redeeming chapter to his life, as he does for those who love and follow him.

God with Joseph

Joseph's hardships could make it easy to conclude that God was not with him or there was a flaw in Joseph's faith. Yet the text assures us of what is not obvious: God was with Joseph—working on his behalf, arranging circumstances, and guiding his life. Genesis says, "The LORD was *with Joseph*. . . . His master saw that the LORD was *with him*. . . . Joseph found favor. . . . But the LORD was *with Joseph* and showed him steadfast love. . . . The LORD was *with him*" (39:2–4, 21, 23).

The text could not be more clear. God was with Joseph.

Though these verses may feel like Joseph's highlight reel, his trial was not over. More hardship and hurt are woven through this same chapter.

While Joseph was working for Potiphar, Potiphar's wife falsely accused Joseph of seducing her. Truth be told, she was seducing him—grabbing his coat as he fled. She used that coat as evidence against Joseph, and Potiphar believed her. Any success Joseph had gained in Potiphar's house vaporized as Joseph found himself in yet another pit—prison.

Though Joseph faced a setback, the text is careful to remind us that Joseph "was there in prison. But the LORD was with Joseph" (vv. 20–21). Joseph was not alone. The Lord was with him, as he had always been—and as he is with you.

Brokenness and Trust

Though Joseph was in prison, God's presence and favor enabled him to interpret Pharaoh's dreams of coming abundance followed by famine. And as a result, Joseph transitioned to a place of position and prominence—second-in-command over Egypt.

All was well, right? Not exactly. Though Joseph had success and status, the pain of his brothers' rejection still stung. That pain resurfaced when Joseph encountered his brothers again after so many years.

Before we watch God's plan unfold, I want us to pause and consider the hurt that weighed on Joseph's heart. The sorrow in his soul. Though Joseph had outward success, he wrestled inwardly.

Have you been there? Wounded by a parent, spouse, child, employer, sibling, or friend? Sometimes it can feel like the Enemy has stolen someone (or something) from you that you once considered God's gift.

And yet here's what I find so unique about Joseph.

He wept. Seven times in the text, Joseph wept over his situation.[1]

As I reflect on Joseph's emotional response, I think of times when, as a little girl, I would come home after a day of being teased and feeling rejected by friends. Perhaps I was an overly sensitive kid, but some days seemed unbearable. Their words stung. I would do my best to hold myself together and fight back the tears, telling myself to be strong.

But once I arrived home, everything changed. Mom would ask about my day, and I'd fall apart. My burden of hurt released like a broken dam as I shared the day's events. Mom's loving presence was a safe place to release my pain. The mingling of her love and my vulnerability made my heart whole.

How similar to our heavenly Father.

When the world hurls its fiercest blows, we do our best to remain strong and move forward. Fighting thoughts of failure, inadequacy, and fear, we continue with work, family, friendships, and service. But when we experience our heavenly Father's presence and his love's touch, everything changes. Our hearts soften. God's love comforts us like the tender love of a mother's embrace. His presence is a safe place to release pain, hurt, and disappointment.

> **When we experience our heavenly Father's presence and his love's touch, everything changes. Our hearts soften.**

Like a fearful or hurt child who breaks into tears of relief and joy at the sight of his mother, so it is when we're touched by our heavenly Father.

In his presence, everything changes.

Our culture teaches us to numb the pain, doesn't it? *Buy this, eat that, indulge here, scroll here, achieve this.* But God's love overshadows any attempt to hold ourselves together. In his presence we can release our emotions and experience his touch. Through his love, we are made whole.

Joseph's raw emotion is an invaluable lesson for me. It doesn't indicate a lack of faith or the absence of God's presence. Instead, it's in vulnerability and brokenness where God's touch is the sweetest, where the deepest healing occurs.

Let Joseph's example of brokenness and trust etch in your heart. God was not finished with Joseph, nor is he finished with you or me.

Day 7 | Joseph: God Meant It for Good

The Bigger Plan

Joseph's new position as second-in-command in Egypt involved preparing the nation for the coming famine. This was all strategic in God's plan. When the famine arrived, Joseph's brothers traveled to Egypt for food. Little did they know their travels would bring them face-to-face with Joseph after years of separation.

Are you seeing the pieces fit together? Do you see a divine plan?

When Joseph's brothers arrived in Egypt, Joseph recognized them, but they did not know him. Initially choosing to conceal his identity, Joseph waited to reveal himself until the brothers had returned for food several times. Finally the time had arrived.

If Joseph's life were a movie, the music would swell at this scene, and we'd all be grabbing our tissues. I've included the text so we can soak in the moving moment. "Joseph could not control himself before all those who stood by him. . . . And he wept aloud, so that the Egyptians heard it, and the household of Pharaoh heard it. . . . And he said, 'I am your brother, Joseph, whom you sold into Egypt'" (Gen. 45:1–2, 4).

Picture the scene. Joseph is standing before his brothers, the same brothers who had stripped him of his father's robe, left him in a pit without water, and sold him to traders. It was a rejection that initiated years of separation from his family, false accusation, and unjust imprisonment. Yet now, the dreams he had so long ago were being fulfilled before his eyes.

A flood of emotion overtook Joseph like a fierce force. He could not hold himself together and wept with such intensity that Pharaoh's house and the Egyptians heard it. However, Joseph's heart was not without hope. His faith was strong.

How do we know? Through the words he spoke next: "Do not be angry with yourselves for selling me here, because it was to save lives that God sent me ahead of you" (v. 5 NIV).

Catch the lens through which Joseph was looking. Despite the rejection, Joseph said it was *God*, not his brothers, who sent him to Egypt. Again, Joseph said: "God sent me ahead of you . . . to save your lives" (v. 7 NIV).

Joseph's confidence in God's sovereignty carried him through this emotional moment and the years of separation. God hadn't lost control. He wasn't pacing the floors of heaven or wringing his hands in frustration. Rather, God was working to perform something extraordinary in Joseph's life.

Through Joseph's words, we also grasp God's greater plan for Joseph in Egypt: *to save lives.*

Let me put this together. God revealed the coming famine to Joseph and placed him second-in-command to store food for the country. When the famine came, Egypt had enough food to sustain people from around the world, including Joseph's brothers. Joseph saved lives by supplying food to millions who may have perished due to the famine.

But if we stop here, we miss the most profound detail: God had promised Abraham, Isaac, and Jacob that the Seed—Jesus—would come through their family. If not for the provision Joseph's family received through his preparation in Egypt, they could have perished in the famine! More specifically, Joseph's brother Judah—whose family line birthed the Messiah—could have died (Gen. 49:10). Amazing.

Joseph kept the line of the Offspring—through whom God promised all the nations would be blessed—alive. What man meant for evil God used to advance his plan. Joseph said it best: "You meant evil against me, but God meant it for good, to bring it about that many people should be kept alive" (Gen. 50:20).

To keep people alive. What a story! Joseph endured theft, betrayal, neglect, exploitation, relocation, sexual temptation, false accusation, and imprisonment. Though broken, Joseph looked through the lens that believed God would take Joseph's hardship and script a bigger story.

And in some mysterious way, it's as if Joseph accepted it as God's plan (Gen. 45:5, 7). But this acceptance wasn't apathy. Joseph pressed on with diligence and integrity. In the end, his stellar response propelled him to a place of deliverance—not only for himself but for millions and, ultimately, for the Seed who would come.

Asking the Right Question
God has given us stories like Joseph's and others' not to fill words on a page but to fill our hearts with hope. From them we can learn that God wants us to trust him. He wants us to look through the lens of faith, even when we don't understand his plan—a lesson we've learned through our journey.

Noah obeyed when he didn't understand and constructed a massive boat.

Abraham left his hometown in obedience, not knowing why or where he was going. He trusted God for a child even when it was physically impossible. Then he offered that child, Isaac, in faith when it seemed to contradict God's plan.

Joseph had to continue moving forward, even when the straight line of God's plan was a tangled mess in the eyes of man.

And yet in each of these situations, God fulfilled his promise. Noah's ark saved his family from a catastrophic flood. God gave Abraham and Sarah a son and provided a ram in Isaac's place. God used the tragedy in Joseph's life to preserve the line through which the Messiah would come.

As for you and me, God invites us to a relationship of trust, resting on his promise that "for those who love God all things work together for good" (Rom. 8:28).

Truth and Trust

What if God's goal for you right now is not a quick escape from the hurt and uncertainty but a relationship of trust? A dependence where you know he will work things for good in his perfect time. A posture where you come before him with your needs and desires, knowing he hears and responds to your cry (Ps. 34:17). What if God wants you to see through a lens of faith?

Rest in the knowledge that he has allowed the events of your life— even the test you are facing right now—to bring you to deeper trust and faith in him (1 Peter 1:6–7). It's okay if you don't understand the specifics of every situation or always have answers.

It's easy to get caught in the trap of asking why. *Why me? Why now? Why did this happen?* But we don't see Joseph asking why, at least not aloud or through his actions. I think Joseph may have asked another question: What?

God, what do you want me to do with this situation?

What do I need to learn about you through this trial?

When we replace *why* with *what*, we are reminded that God doesn't waste our pain. There's a divine purpose behind what perplexes us, and this perspective can pull us from despair.

For the questions in your mind today, could you simply ask God, "What would you have me do in this situation? What do I need to know about you? What do you want me to see?"

Sometimes, even the questions must settle. We must live one day at a time, one moment at a time, surrendering to his plan and in relationship with him, knowing his grace is sufficient for every situation (2 Cor. 12:9).

Find comfort in this: God is with you, even now. He has a perspective you do not have. He sees what you cannot see. You can rest, knowing he's scripting a bigger story for you and those you love.

Don't dismiss the part of you deep down that wants to trust—wants to believe that God will work out this situation for good. Don't let the fears and questions push away the peace your heart can know and desperately needs.

Trust in God.
Hold to his promises.
Obey what he has said.
This is the path to peace.

Questions

What about Joseph's journey stands out to you most?

How have you seen God work challenging circumstances in ways that turned for good?

How does the truth of God's sovereignty change how you view your current struggles?

How might your attitude be different if you really believed God works hard times out for good?

Learning from the example of Joseph, how can you let hard times strengthen, not stifle you?

JESSE TREE

What is something you want to remember about Joseph's story and how God meant it for good?

TRACING
HIS
Provision
THROUGH
MOSES

Day 8

PASSOVER:
DIVINE DELIVERANCE

Read Exodus 12:1–31.

Soon after becoming an empty nester, my mom read the great Christian classic *The Practice of the Presence of God* by Brother Lawrence. It's a book that reminds Christians of God's nearness and encourages them to live in relationship with him—whether doing their dishes or praying on their knees. Mom loved the idea so much that she began practicing the presence of God in her everyday life. And so naturally, being a woman who enjoys a good sale, a shopping day with Jesus ensued.

TRACING HIS PROVISION THROUGH MOSES

On the morning of their venture, Mom walked Jesus to the garage, where she opened the passenger door for him and fastened his seat belt. During the car ride, they had the best of conversations. Once at the mall, she helped Jesus out of the car, and off they went, practically hand in hand.

A few hours later, Mom walked Jesus back to the parking lot, and they made a quick trip to Wendy's. There, they enjoyed more conversation. After lunch it was back to the mall for more shopping. But after an hour in the mall, Mom's stomach dropped, and she gasped. *Oh no! I left Jesus . . . at Wendy's!*

I'm not sure if Mom went back to Wendy's to get Jesus. Here's what I do know: There was no need. Jesus wasn't sitting at Wendy's, peering out the window and waiting for a ride. He was with her at that moment as much as he'd been earlier that morning.

It's easy to limit God's presence to certain places, isn't it? Though we can experience God's love and presence corporately in dynamic ways, we often limit him to those places. And if we're honest, when facing difficulty, we may not feel him at all and wonder if he's there.

Like what my mom learned on her shopping trip and what we must remember: We don't have to consciously bring God with us. He goes with us. He's already there. But if we're not consciously paying attention, we will not see him.

As the story of God's people unfolds, we'll see that God is with them, guiding their steps and providing for their needs. And as we see God's presence and provision in their lives, we'll be encouraged of his in our own. He is with us. And every obstacle—big or small—is an opportunity to trust an unfailing, ever-present God.

Day 8 | Passover: Divine Deliverance

Today we study Passover, a pivotal event when the Hebrew people experienced God's presence through divine protection and deliverance from Egyptian bondage. It's a thrilling story where we see an Old Testament picture of the coming Christ unlike anywhere else.

The Prayer God Heard

We finished yesterday's study by looking at Joseph and his brothers in Egypt. What began as one family's search for food evolved into a residence of four hundred years and a family multiplying into a massive nation.

However, life for the Hebrews took a sharp turn when a new pharaoh, who knew nothing of Joseph, came to power. Egypt became a hostile and oppressive place. Pharaoh, threatened by their growing population, decreed a horrific act: cast every newborn Hebrew boy into the river.

Not only was this abhorrent, but it has profound significance within the broader picture of Scripture, specifically concerning the promised Seed. To this point in our study, the Seed has survived a catastrophic flood, dueling brothers, family conflict, and a severe famine. Now due to Pharaoh's mandate, the threat against the Seed is further intensified. Man sought to destroy the Seed, but God would move heaven and earth to preserve his people and, above all, the Seed.

Before we look at God's miraculous deliverance, I want to encourage you with a phrase that strikes me in this story. Exodus 2 describes the people's desperation and how they called out to God for deliverance: "The people of Israel groaned because of their slavery. . . . Their cry for rescue from slavery came up to God" (v. 23).

Their cry "came up" to God. Does this resonate with you as it does me? Sure, God is with us, and our prayers don't travel to a location.

Still, I love the picture this phrase provides. In desperation, the people cried out to God and their prayers ascended to him.

If you're like me, you may cry out to God and then question if he heard. Your need was urgent. The pain was real. Still, you wonder, *God, did you hear me? Will you answer?* Yet the text assures us of what we often doubt. God "heard their groaning." Not only that, he heard and "remembered his covenant with Abraham" (v. 24).

God had not forgotten the covenant. This word *covenant* should grab our attention. The covenant in Exodus was the same covenant he had made with Abraham in Genesis 15 (day 4). A promise that included not only the Seed but possession of *land* (Gen. 15:18–21).

Catch this profound connection. At this point in history, God's people were not living in the land God had promised to Abraham and his descendants. Not hardly. They had been calling Egypt home for more than four hundred years—and under the new pharaoh, life had become oppressive. Rather than sit back and think this was meant to be, the people cried out to God for help. And God—on the foundation of his promise—would move on their behalf.

Can this be a reminder to you and me? How often do we say we believe God yet doubt his ability? How quickly do we forget we have promises on which to stand? I know I do. But the people of Israel refocused their frustration and cried out to God.

Is there something you need from God and you're wondering if he's heard? A child who needs his touch. Struggles with mental health. Conflict at work. Wisdom for the care of aging parents. Relational tensions. Peace or self-control.

Be confident of this: prayer sets the divine and miraculous work of

God in motion. When you or I pray about a specific situation, we invite the presence of God and the activity of the Holy Spirit into that situation in a way they would not have been unless we prayed.

> ## Prayer sets the divine and miraculous work of God in motion.

Though our feelings may tell us differently, God hears the cry of those who call on him (Ps. 145:18). As with the Israelites, our prayers go up to God. The answer may be delayed or look different from what we anticipated. Still, God heard their prayer, as he does ours.

The Night God Passed Over

God answered the people's cry by raising up Moses. What makes me smile about Moses is his obvious weakness and inability from the start. I suspect he may have had a few anger issues, struggled through public speaking in high school, and probably wasn't asking God for a national deliverance ministry.

But as God beautifully does, he moved in Moses's life and chose this insecure underdog to face off against Pharaoh.

Under God's direction, Moses asked Pharaoh to let the people leave Egypt. No surprise, Pharaoh would not have it. In response God delivered a series of plagues, but Pharaoh's heart remained rock-hard.

With the tenth plague God would bring unparalleled judgment on all of Egypt: "I will strike all the firstborn in the land of Egypt, both man and beast; and on all the gods of Egypt I will execute judgments: I am the LORD" (Exod. 12:12).

Are you seeing this? God would kill *every* firstborn. Imagine the devastation.

I read this judgment and think of the street where I live. As I consider the families around me, I cannot fathom the grief that would sweep our street if every firstborn child perished in one night. And that's just my street. What if we walked through our neighborhoods, towns, and cities and imagined every home waking to the sudden and unexpected death of the firstborn child?

The heartbreak is unthinkable. And yet in the middle of this horror and judgment, there was *one* thing that could prevent death and stop the sweep of death. Would it be physical barriers? Strong military? An army of heavenly hosts?

No. A lamb.

A soft, white, fluffy lamb. More specifically, blood from that lamb. A sacrifice.

To avoid the death of their firstborns, God instructed each Hebrew household to kill an unblemished male lamb and brush its blood on the doorframe. The blood would serve as a sign, or distinguishing mark, setting that house apart from the others. With those instructions, God said: "When I see the blood, I will *pass over* you, and no plague will befall you to destroy you" (v. 13).

At midnight God swept through Egypt with this final plague, striking every firstborn in homes without the blood and *passing over* homes marked with the blood of the lamb. It was the night of "Passover."

With God's sweeping judgment, Pharaoh's resistance shattered. He summoned Moses and Aaron by night and ordered them out of Egypt.

Day 8 | Passover: Divine Deliverance

This was their deliverance! After years of oppression, the Hebrew people fled Egypt and began their journey to the land of promise.[1] God had heard their cry.

The New Testament Connection

The Passover event was such a defining moment for God's people that he commanded them to remember it every year (Exod. 12:24–27). This annual celebration would be like our Fourth of July, Thanksgiving, or Christmas—a time when people collectively look back to a significant event. Because of God's command, every year at the time of Passover, Jewish communities were to gather and recall the night their ancestors escaped Pharaoh's hand by the blood of the lamb.

What thrills me is how this annual celebration of Passover connects to Jesus. During a Passover celebration fifteen hundred years after the original Passover, Jesus went to a hill called Calvary and shed his blood for the salvation of the world!

In fact, Scripture tells us Jesus's last meal with the disciples was a Passover meal (Luke 22:8, 15). The significance was undeniable and breathtaking: Jesus is the lamb. Every previous Passover celebration had looked forward to the moment when God chose *his* lamb to be the sacrifice for the world.

That's why John called Jesus the "Lamb of God, who takes away the sin of the world" (John 1:29). That's why Revelation calls Jesus the "Lamb who was slain" (5:12; 13:8). And that's why Paul said, "Christ, our Passover lamb, has been sacrificed" (1 Cor. 5:7).

As the blood of lambs brought salvation from God's judgment in Egypt, so the blood of Jesus grants us freedom from God's coming judgment on the earth. It's a profound picture of salvation for those who believe.

Deeds on the Door

As I was studying Passover, a thought came to mind. What if an Israelite had used something other than lamb's blood on the door? What if they thought, *Kill a lamb? How about I sacrifice this pigeon and then tack a list of my good deeds to the door instead. That should work.*

The error is obvious. Yet how often do we hear that good works satisfy a holy God? Or how many people think being a good person grants entrance to heaven? Perhaps you have believed the same thing.

Scripture is clear: good works are not good enough (Rom 3:20; Gal. 2:16). We shouldn't believe our good works satisfy God any more than the Israelites should have believed pigeon's blood and a list of good deeds would have satisfied God's judgment the night of Passover.

From a human perspective, brushing blood on a doorframe to escape judgment doesn't make sense. And yet in the economy of God, faith in the sacrifice and shedding of Jesus's blood is the only way to know salvation and be free from eternal punishment (John 5:24; Acts 4:12). Our salvation, like that of the Israelites on the night of Passover, depends on whether we trust in his work or our own.

The good news is, we don't have to live up to a perfect standard or earn God's love and acceptance through good deeds. We don't have to strain, hoping we are good enough for heaven. Ephesians says it is "by grace you have been saved through faith. And this is not your own doing; it is the gift of God" (2:8). Salvation is received, not achieved. Our response is to accept his work on our behalf and know we are saved by God's perfect lamb—Jesus Christ.

Truth and Trust

Let this reminder encourage your heart: This was all God's plan and under his sovereign control. The time in Egypt. The oppression. The miraculous deliverance. Jesus's coming. Jesus's death. His resurrection. All in his plan and all for his purpose.

The apostle Peter told us that God chose Jesus before the foundation of the world (1 Peter 1:20). Not only that, in the Abrahamic covenant, God foretold Israel's coming slavery, their deliverance, and the precise length of their time there (Gen. 15:13–14).

When you find yourself in a season of uncertainty, know that your future is in God's knowledge and loving hand. The spouse or friend you've been praying for, the interview you have tomorrow, the child you need help raising, the son or daughter you just started home-schooling, or the aging parent who has you concerned. God is holding all things together, and his timing is perfect.

At the same time, we don't need to sit in passivity. When we cry out to God, our prayer goes up to him. As we pray, we can walk assured of his provision and presence in our lives.

> He hears our cry.
> His sacrifice is enough.
> And he is with you.

Questions

The people *cried out* to God for deliverance, and God heard their cry. Recall a time in your life when you knew God heard your cry and answered your prayer.

Is there a situation you can be lifting up to God now?

Do you ever find yourself leaning on good works to satisfy God or get his attention? In what ways?

Only the blood of Christ makes us right with God. How does this truth impact you personally?

JESSE TREE

What is something you want to remember about the Passover lamb?

Day 9

THE LAW:
WHAT WE COULD NEVER DO

Read Exodus 19:10–25; 20:1–19.

*H*ave you ever hosted a birthday party for kids and about halfway through thought, *I should have set some rules from the beginning?* Kids are climbing the furniture, wrestling, throwing food, and slamming doors. You get the idea.

If you've been around children or have your own, you know the importance of rule setting from the beginning. It's how we communicate expectations and behavior standards. Rules like don't slide down the stairs, write on the walls, or put your friend in a headlock seem to keep the house in order.

Similarly, God is about to begin a new and exciting chapter for his people: life in the promised land. But before they get too far in their newfound freedom, God gives them his standard of behavior—the law. Just as my party rules reflect the standard of conduct for my home, God's law revealed his perfect standard for his people.

Today's study provides a fresh perspective on the Old Testament law and how it leads us to Jesus and the grace he brings.

A Holy Moment

As God's people journeyed from Egypt to the promised land, they camped in the wilderness of Sinai. There, God had Moses prepare the people because in three days his presence would descend on the mountain and he would give the Ten Commandments.

While we may be familiar with the Ten Commandments, it's important to know that God gave many other guidelines as part of the Old Testament law—613, to be precise.[1] Maybe I should try that at my next birthday party!

Why so many laws? God was calling his people to be separate from the world (Exod. 19:5–6). Living by these laws would set them apart as unique people and worshipers of the one true God.

When God gave the Ten Commandments, it wasn't a quick text, email, or DocuSign. He spoke from the mountain to the people. *Audibly.* It was a manifestation of his power unlike anything they had witnessed. "There were thunders and lightnings and a thick cloud . . . so that all the people in the camp trembled. . . . And as the sound of the trumpet grew louder and louder, Moses spoke, and God answered him in thunder. The LORD came down on Mount Sinai" (Exod. 19:16, 19–20).

Day 9 | The Law: What We Could Never Do

Imagine the moment. A mass of people shaking at the sight and sound of thunder, lightning, a trembling mountain, and a trumpet blasting with growing intensity. As I read this, I pause and wonder where the blasting trumpet was and who was playing it. Was it God? An angel? Christ himself? While we don't know the details, the giving of the law was a matchless and memorable display of God's power.

Why such a sight? This was a holy and historic moment in the life of God's people. The law revealed God's holiness and the standard by which his people should live. Not only that, through the law, God established the Mosaic covenant—his basis for interaction with them in the promised land.

Unlike the Abrahamic covenant, the Mosaic covenant was conditional. That is, *if* the people kept the law, they would be blessed and stay in the land. If they ignored the law, God would punish them and remove them from the land (Deut. 11:26–28; 28:58–63).

Or like the birthday party: If you obey, you'll get cake and ice cream. But if you ruin the furniture, you might just go home.

You'll want to tuck the conditional nature of the Mosaic covenant in your mind because throughout our journey, we'll see a connection between the people's behavior and their success or defeat in the promised land.

Connection to Christ

Like Passover, the giving of the law was a jaw-dropping, pinnacle moment. But how does it connect to Christ? The answer is in the words of Jesus himself: "Do not think that I have come to abolish the Law or the Prophets; I have not come to abolish them but to *fulfill* them" (Matt. 5:17). Incredible! What God gave Moses on the mountain is what Christ fulfilled on earth.

But what does this mean? I'll use an everyday example to illustrate. If you or I take out a loan and pay it off, we would say we have *fulfilled* the loan's requirements, having done everything to satisfy the loan. Nothing more needs to be paid.

In the same way, when Jesus lived a sinless life and died as the perfect sacrifice, he fulfilled what the law required, satisfying a holy and perfect God. Because of what Jesus did, nothing else needs to be paid.

Just as we are no longer bound to a loan once it has been fulfilled, we are no longer bound to the Old Testament law because it has been fulfilled through Jesus!

But what about when we feel the need to work for God's love? Or when we get stuck in guilt and condemnation?

Let's say I paid off the loan for my house. But the next day, my son went to the bank with his coin collection and said he wanted to pay the loan. It wouldn't make sense. There would be nothing to pay.

Remember this—Jesus did what we could never do. Through his life, he satisfied God's requirements and fulfilled the law. He paid the debt. Nothing else needs to be paid.

But how often do we feel the need to approach God with our piggy bank of good works, trying to earn his love or make up for what we've done wrong? In Christ, acceptance is received, not achieved. And that acceptance comes when we believe in what Jesus did for us through his death and resurrection.

This is important to remember because the struggle to receive the gift of grace is hard for many. We think, *I've made too many mistakes. I'm not good enough. I'll never get my life together enough for God to love me.*

Can you relate? As I've talked to women, I've found that sometimes we may know God's salvation and forgiveness. And yet there can be regrets from our past that resurface with the stain of shame.

In Christ, acceptance is received, not achieved.

This was the case of a woman who approached me after I had taught on forgiveness. Though a Christian most of her adult life, Leah shared that no matter how hard she tried, she could not shake the shame she felt over a decision from twenty years earlier—unfaithfulness to her husband. Even though Leah had reconciled with her husband and asked God for forgiveness, experiencing that forgiveness seemed impossible.

As the room emptied, Leah and I walked step-by-step through the power of Jesus's forgiveness in a way that shined light into the dark cave of her shame. By the end of our conversation, Leah confessed she felt free from the burden of guilt she'd carried most of her adult life. She realized forgiveness is not of her doing but a gift of grace. And if a holy God could forgive her, how much more could she forgive herself and walk in the sweet peace of his forgiveness?

What Leah recognized is what we must remember. Striving is not needed for acceptance. We don't need to punish ourselves or wallow in guilt to merit God's acceptance.

True forgiveness through Jesus means a release from *every* sin.

Questions About the Law

I love today's study because it reminds us of our forgiveness in Christ. It also clears up confusion surrounding the law in the Old Testament and the law in our lives. Maybe like me, you've wondered, *What does it mean that Jesus satisfied the law? What does the end of the law mean? If we are not under the Old Testament law, what kind of guidelines do we follow?*

For the rest of today, we'll answer these questions in memorable and easy-to-understand ways. I promise some fun along the way too!

Speed Limits and Birthday Parties

As we understand more about the law, it's important we know that nothing about the law gave people the power to obey (Rom. 8:3). It was simply the standard. When teaching about the Old Testament law, I like to compare it to a speed limit sign. A speed limit sign may be posted, but it doesn't give us the ability or desire to obey. It's not going to jump off the road, into our car, and make us slow down. It simply communicates the standard. The same is true of the Old Testament law. It communicated the standard but did not empower people to obey.

Also, the law was never meant as a way of salvation. Paul said, "No one will be declared righteous in God's sight by the works of the law" (Rom. 3:20 NIV). In fact, the law contains no provision for heaven or eternal life.

You may wonder, *If the law didn't give the power to obey or give eternal life, what did it do?* Paul anticipated that question and provided a profound answer: "Why, then, was the law given? It was given alongside the promise to *show people their sins*" (Gal. 3:19 NLT).

Day 9 | The Law: What We Could Never Do

We could think of the birthday party to illustrate. Let's say when the kids arrived, I posted 613 rules on my refrigerator. Then after the party, we compared the rules against their behavior. By doing this, the list of 613 rules would *show* the kids what they did wrong. In the same way, the law *shows* people their sins.

Notice what else Paul said. The law came "alongside" the promise to Abraham. The law did not replace God's promise to Abraham regarding the coming Christ. Rather, the law and the promise to Abraham coexisted.

Paul continued by saying how long the law would last: "But the law was designed to last only until the coming of the child who was promised" (v. 19 NLT). Are you seeing this? The law lasted "only until" the child came who was promised. In other words, the law lasted *until* Jesus. With Jesus came "the end of the law for righteousness to everyone who believes" (Rom. 10:4).

The End of the Law

I admit that talking about the law "ending" can raise many questions. I'll explain with a fun and final illustration.

Because of our family's moves, our children have changed schools several times. One transition was from an Arizona school to a Virginia school. When we were in Arizona, the kids were under the rules of that school. When we left, they were no longer under those rules. Things like lunchtimes, school uniforms, and hall passes became obsolete. Once in Virginia, they were under a new set of rules.

The Old Testament law is holy, righteous, and good (Rom. 7:12). However, like the Arizona school, it was for a specific time and people. It was what God's people followed *until* Christ came. But since you and

I live after Jesus fulfilled and ended the law, we are no longer under the Old Testament law. We have changed schools, so to speak.

Now, for the rebels out there (you know who you are), this does not mean we're without a standard. We are now under the standard of behavior presented in the New Testament. We follow the high standard of Jesus's teaching and New Testament doctrine—all summarized by Jesus in the two greatest commandments: love God and love others as yourself (Matt. 22:36–40).

Are there similarities and overlaps between the Old and New Testament standards? Absolutely. Just like there were similar rules in the Arizona and Virginia schools. In fact, when Jesus taught the law in the Sermon on the Mount, he called people to an even higher standard of holiness through actions and heart (Matt. 5–7). Therefore, when looking to the standard we should follow, we obey the words of Christ and the New Testament teachings.

What we must remember is whether we're speaking of the Old Testament law or the New Testament teachings, no one keeps the law perfectly. No one keeps the 613 rules on the refrigerator. We all fall short, which leads us to our final reason for the law.

Truth and Trust
Paul explained a final purpose of the law that ties our lesson together: "So then, the law was our guardian until Christ came, in order that we might be justified by faith" (Gal. 3:24).

Think of what a tutor or guardian does. They train us and teach us what's right and wrong—like the rules on the refrigerator or someone supervising the party. In the same way, Paul said the law served as a guardian, showing right from wrong.

Day 9 | The Law: What We Could Never Do

The law could never make us perfect or give us eternal life. Instead, it takes us by the hand and points to the perfect One. The law doesn't save but leads to the Savior, so we can be justified by faith.

Do you see how this all comes together? The Old Testament law did not replace the promise of the coming Seed. It was added *alongside* God's promise to Abraham.

But the law lasted until Jesus—the promised Seed—came. The Old Testament law ended with Jesus because he fulfilled what the law required (Matt. 5:17; Rom. 10:4). Therefore, we are no longer under the Old Testament law but under the standard of Jesus's words and the New Testament teachings.

And the law's purpose? To show us our sins and lead us to the Savior!

It's why God sent the perfect Son to fulfill the law and take away the sin of the world (John 1:29). And that's why we, like Leah, can know the sweet peace of his forgiveness and a loving relationship with him.

If I could whisper something into your heart today, it would be this: No matter what you've done, there is forgiveness through Jesus. *Completely.* You don't need to sit in guilt and shame, burdened by the weight of regrets and what-ifs. You don't need to spend your days re-hashing your mistakes or allowing gnawing guilt to steal your joy.

Jesus did what we could never do. The debt is paid. Grace and truth came through Jesus.

The next time you feel the arrows of shame and guilt, place yourself under God's grace with your thoughts.

You are free.
You are forgiven.
You are loved.
Jesus paid it all.

Questions

Have you ever felt like you needed to do more for God to forgive you?

How does the idea of Jesus fulfilling the law bring rest to your heart?

In what ways does this chapter help you understand the law's purpose?

How could you summarize the purpose of the law in a sentence or two?

Is there something from your past that still carries the sting of guilt? How could focusing on Jesus's sacrifice and God's forgiveness help you let go of the guilt you carry?

JESSE TREE

What is something you want to remember about the law?

Day 10

JOSHUA:
FAITH OVER FEELING

Read Numbers 13:25–14:9.

I was a music major in college but never dreamed I'd make it into one of the school's most popular choirs as the assistant pianist. Surprisingly, I did. With tours, travel, and recording projects, it was *the* choir to be in.

But there was a problem. This was a gospel choir where the musicians played by ear, and my training had been strictly classical. I was the type of pianist who could read anything put in front of me. But play a song by ear? *Impossible.* And honestly, terrifying.

This was especially unsettling because every rehearsal opened with the accompanist playing a song the director chose on the spot. Since the main pianist could play by ear and I was the assistant, it didn't seem to be a problem. But I always feared the day the pianist would be absent and I'd be asked to play in his place.

Two months into the semester, that day came.

As rehearsal was starting, the accompanist popped out of the room. The choir director motioned me to come to the grand piano. He cued me to begin playing, and in his booming voice said, "Good evening, choir. Let's sing the old hymn 'Amazing Grace.'"

I panicked. *"Amazing Grace"? Shouldn't every church pianist know how to play "Amazing Grace"?*

Feeling the blood rush to my face, I shook my head no because the words would. Not. Come. Then in front of the 150-voice choir, the director stared at me in shock and said, "You *can't* play 'Amazing Grace'?"

"No . . . no, I can't," I muttered, feeling so small.

I returned to my chair, buried my face in my hands, and sobbed.

No surprise, that was my last semester in choir. No one asked me to leave. I didn't pray about my decision or talk with anyone. I just quit. Though God had opened this door of opportunity, I doubted my ability and let those feelings win.

Live by Fear or Let Faith Win

Our fears and feelings have the potential to control and cripple us. They can quench creativity, complicate relationships, choke dreams, and steal the joy of everyday life. At an even deeper level, our feelings can chip away at our faith. Rather than move forward with the confidence that God is with us, we cave under our thoughts and fears. As a result, we live a "less than" life because we let our feelings win.

This was the case for the people of Israel as they neared the promised land.

Moses had sent twelve spies into the area. At first, the spies returned with grand descriptions of the land, evidenced by a grape cluster so large it required two burly men to carry. But the spies returned with something else: a bad report. And the mood turned sour. The land, though lush, teemed with giants and fortified cities.

> Our fears and feelings have the potential to control and cripple us.

The people faced a decision: live by faith or let fear win. Their response? "If only we had *died* in Egypt! Or in this wilderness! Why is the LORD bringing us to this land only to let us fall by the sword? . . . We should choose a leader and go back to Egypt" (Num. 14:2–4 NIV).

Do you sense their despair? Notice the people's response went beyond complaining to attacking the character of God. They asked, "Why is God bringing us into the land to kill us?" As if God were playing some cruel trick of delivering them from Egypt only to let them perish in the wilderness.

God's plan was harder than they'd expected.

Have you ever noticed this can be a common experience when walking with God? We pray for something to happen, yet living it out can be surprisingly difficult. Sometimes God stretches us to a point where it feels we can't take another step. The problem appears insurmountable, and we're tempted to quit.

We remember the simpler days of the past and long for their comfort. When we consider the future, rather than delighting in God's promises, dread fills our hearts. Even the lightest tasks carry the heaviest weight.

Does this sound familiar? Perhaps you've suffered a recent loss, and each day is a struggle. Maybe your spouse's faith has fallen flat, and it impacts your marriage and kids. Perhaps you're in the process of fostering or adopting and the sacrifice feels too great. You want to believe God but aren't sure how and if you can.

Here's what I find fascinating about the Israelites' disbelief. This generation had *just* experienced the miraculous escape from Egypt. Think about it. Hadn't they'd killed the lambs, spread blood over their doorframes, and experienced the miracle of Passover? Hadn't they'd walked through the Red Sea on dry land and witnessed God's presence on Mount Sinai?

God had delivered them in the past. Would he not deliver them now? The truth was, he would. That was his promise! The people were approaching the same land God had promised to Abraham and his descendants in the Abrahamic covenant (day 4, Gen. 15). If that wasn't enough, God had assured Moses, "I am giving [this land] to the people of Israel" (Num. 13:2).

"I am giving."

This was the truth. This was God's plan. They didn't need to question God's directive, focus on their deficiencies, or let fear win. Nor do we. They needed to believe, trust, and move forward in faith.

God was good, and he would provide.

Perceiving and Believing

Have you ever noticed how two people can see the same thing yet perceive the situation differently? For example, my kids spot a roller coaster, and their eyes dance with excitement. I see the same coaster, and I'm searching for the closest park bench.

The Israelites were no different. Though the majority sank in despair, two spies surfaced with a fresh perspective. They said, "The land . . . is an exceedingly good land. If the LORD delights in us, he will bring us into this land. . . . The LORD is with us; do not fear them" (Num. 14:7–9).

Here's what we can't miss. Joshua and Caleb saw the struggle differently. The same land the people said "devours its inhabitants" (13:32) was what Joshua and Caleb called "exceedingly good." The people believed God was absent, but Joshua and Caleb said the "LORD is with us." What others viewed as an obstacle, Joshua and Caleb saw as an opportunity to trust a faithful God.

But sadly, their faith didn't spark hope in the people. Just the opposite. Rather than rally behind these two men of faith, the people discussed ways to murder them. *Murder.* With the people's horrific intent, God stepped in with a strong judgment—death on everyone twenty years

and older. He said, "In this wilderness your bodies will fall—every one
... who has grumbled against me" (14:29 NIV).

Intense, isn't it? What I find most sobering are the chilling words God
used to pronounce the judgment—words that would have sounded
strangely familiar to the people. God announced: "I will do to you the
very thing I *heard* you say" (v. 28 NIV).

What did God mean? What had the people said? When the people
first saw the land, they complained, "If only we had *died* in Egypt! Or
in this wilderness!" (v. 2 NIV). And now, in this wilderness, they would
fall. And here's the irony. Their deaths wouldn't come by the giants
they feared most. It would come through the discipline of God.

God would strike with the words they had spoken.

I don't know about you, but this arrests my attention. How easily we
complain about our lives—our problems, struggles, and setbacks. I'm
not saying God will strike us dead, but through this story we see how
seriously God viewed their unbelief regarding his goodness and his
promise.

Here's what you and I must remember: we can trust God's character,
his goodness, and his ability to provide. God hasn't brought you where
you are to betray you. He is good and gracious. Whether you're simply
trying to live day to day or you're facing the biggest challenge of your
life, God will give you the strength you need. Our job is to lift our
prayers to him and follow his directive.

The Director's Perspective

Three years after quitting the choir, I ran into the assistant choir director on campus. After chatting for a while, he surprised me by asking me why I had quit. I shared my reasons, to which he responded

with an answer that still impacts me to this day: "Do you know what the director told me after you left? He said you would have been the best accompanist the choir ever had."

Me. The girl who couldn't play "Amazing Grace."

I'll never forget how I felt in that moment. I was grateful for the encouragement yet felt deep loss and regret as I realized what I'd missed because I had let fear win. At the same time, I knew I had learned a lesson that would stay with me for the rest of my life: what we believe about ourselves and how we view God sets the trajectory of our lives. Will we pull back in fear or move forward in faith? Will we believe what we see, or cling to what God says?

> What we believe about ourselves
> and how we view God sets the
> trajectory of our lives.

As long as we're in this world, we have an Enemy prowling at our heels, wanting to derail us from God's best and the fullness of peace. He twists the truth, makes us doubt God's goodness, and trips us up with illusions of inadequacy and lies of defeat. The Enemy wants us to follow his path and stay stuck in the wilderness, peering into the promises but never walking in.

But God has more.

What is the situation you're facing now—the one keeping you stuck in the wilderness, the one stealing your joy and consuming your thoughts? In your struggle and mine, what if we stopped long enough to see ourselves and our situations through God's eyes and not our own? What if we viewed our situations not as obstacles but as opportunities to trust God?

What if we lived with a different perspective?

Joshua and Caleb saw themselves as God did—recipients of the promise. It was a matter of perspective. And because they perceived themselves and their problems differently, they moved forward in faith.

A Picture of Christ

There's an interesting side note to this story I can't let slip past. In the list of the twelve spies' names, Joshua experiences a name change: "Moses gave Hoshea son of Nun the name Joshua" (Num. 13:16 NIV).

Name changes are significant in the Bible. When a name changes, it's often because God wants to convey a message through someone's life or identity. There's something new God desires to do in them or through them.

We see that in Joshua. Joshua's old name, Hoshea, means "salvation." But his new name, Joshua, means "Yahweh is salvation"[1] or God is salvation. No longer would Joshua be called "salvation." God was about to prove that salvation doesn't come through man's strength but through God alone.

What's more, Joshua's name in Greek is translated "Jesus." In the book of Joshua, we see Joshua leading his people into the land of promise—a picture of Jesus, who leads us into a place of salvation and walking in God's promises.[2]

Truth and Trust

As we end this chapter, I want to give you something you can start practicing today—something I'm learning to do in those moments

135

when my feelings want to win: *respond* thoughtfully; don't *react* impulsively.

When faced with a situation, we can either *react* in fear or *respond* in faith.

Reactions are impulsive, faithless, and sometimes foolish. I know I'm reacting when the first thing I feel is overwhelmed and incapable—that part of me that wants to turn back, complain, envision the worst, expect failure, or ask why.

Responses are different. They're faith filled and tempered by God's Word. This is when we view obstacles as opportunities, focusing on the promise, not the problem. Responses mean we process the struggles but do not get stuck in them.

When we respond in faith, we rise above the challenge because we know God is good. Rather than worry, we cover our situation in prayer and trust God for the outcome. We don't grow weary in doing good because we know a reward is coming (Gal. 6:9; Heb. 11:6). Rather than dread the days before us, we delight that God is with us.

What if today, rather than *reacting* in fear, you *responded* in faith? And when God looks at your life and mine, he will describe us as he did his servant Caleb: someone who "has a different spirit and has followed me fully" (Num. 14:24).

Living by faith, not fear.
Seeing opportunities rather than obstacles.
Clinging to God's promise.
Trusting him fully.

Think of a challenge you are currently facing. How could this obstacle be an opportunity to trust God?

Have you ever felt like God promised you something and it required a step of faith to receive it? How did you respond?

Do you often find yourself dreading the future? How could you turn that dread into delight?

How is God encouraging you through the story of Joshua and Caleb? Give a specific example.

JESSE TREE
What is something you want to remember about Joshua and Caleb?

Day 11

RUTH:
REFUGE IN THE
KINSMAN-REDEEMER

Read Ruth 1; 4:13–22.

I 'll never forget the day we rushed our three-year-old daughter to the emergency room. Charity had been suffering from pneumonia and had developed severe abdominal pain. Though the doctors had repeatedly assured us the pain was from her cough, we feared there was something more.

Day 11 | Ruth: Refuge in the Kinsman-Redeemer

Once at the hospital, our suspicions were confirmed: Charity's appendix had burst. The terrifying news only got worse. Because of Charity's pneumonia, performing surgery on her tiny body carried life-threatening risks.

We were desperate.

After a night drenched in prayer and concern, the next morning brought hope. Charity's lungs had improved just enough to operate. We went forward with surgery, inwardly rehearsing the what-ifs. *What if this is a mistake? What if Charity doesn't make it?*

Thankfully, after Charity's surgery and a long week of fighting complications, Ryan and I walked out the hospital doors with our daughter in our arms. I view my now-adult daughter as a living miracle who survived a desperate situation.

Today we will see a different kind of desperate situation. A woman named Naomi lived in Bethlehem when famine struck. In search of relief, Naomi fled to Moab with her husband and two sons. But things only became worse. She experienced the devastating death of her husband, followed by the loss of her two sons.

Widowed. Bereaved of both children. Poor. Alone. Desperate.

Feeling Forsaken

Have you ever noticed how people respond differently to trials? Some place blame, while others assume blame. Some boil in anger, while others withdraw. Some process verbally, and others suffer in silence. Sometimes we can be a messy mix of all the above.

The book of Ruth reveals how Naomi responded. She told the women around her, "Do not call me Naomi; call me Mara, for the Almighty has dealt very *bitterly* with me" (1:20).

What makes this name change so significant? *Naomi* means "pleasant" and *Mara* means "bitter."[1] Notice what's happening in her heart. This tragedy so shook Naomi that she chose to be defined by it. Her loss became her identity.

Naomi continued: "Why call me Naomi, when the LORD has testified against me and the Almighty has brought calamity upon me?" (v. 21).

Do you hear the pain and despair in her voice? As much as Naomi wished it weren't her story, no one could bring her husband and sons back.

Naomi's feelings may be familiar. You've carried a burden or sorrow that seemed like more than you could handle. You knew God was there, but he felt distant rather than near, cruel rather than kind. Times of disappointment when you've thought, *Life shouldn't be like this.* Your struggles were so consuming they defined you.

It's easy to let hardship and grief define us. And in the process, we can unknowingly redefine God as distant, unfair, and harsh. We may not outwardly accuse him, as Naomi did, but inwardly we question his kindness. We compare our lives to others and secretly wonder why things are so challenging for us. We become defined by our difficulty. Sometimes we're so weary from the constant drain that we want to give up and stop trying altogether.

If you've ever felt that this is your story—or the story of someone you love—hold this truth hold close to your heart: God had not forsaken Naomi, nor has he forsaken us (Heb. 13:5).

Day 11 | Ruth: Refuge in the Kinsman-Redeemer

As we continue in Naomi's story, we'll see God's answer to Naomi's desperate situation foreshadow who Christ would be to you and me.

One Woman's Decision

After the famine ended, Naomi returned to Bethlehem. And Ruth, one of her widowed daughters-in-law, joined Naomi—a selfless and sacrificial act that set the narrative of hope in motion.

To get the full flavor of Ruth and Naomi's story, I'll quickly explain how the law and culture made provision for people in their situation. The law instructed landowners to leave part of their fields unharvested so the poor could gather leftover grain. The law also said that a widow would marry her husband's closest male relative—a kinsman-redeemer.[2] Though this relationship seems odd to us, the new marriage promised provision and security for the widow.

Let's see how this connects to Ruth and Naomi.

Chapter 2 opens with the poor and widowed Ruth gleaning leftover grain in a field, where she *"happened to come* to the part of the field belonging to Boaz"* (v. 3). Clearly, this was more than coincidence. Boaz *just happened* to be related to Naomi's deceased husband. Because of the blood relationship, Boaz could marry Ruth and be her kinsman-redeemer.

Boaz noticed Ruth's hard work (and perhaps good looks) in the fields and showed her special attention by providing extra food and protection. More importantly, he spoke a blessing over her: "May you be richly rewarded by the LORD, the God of Israel, under whose wings you have come to take refuge" (v. 12 NIV).

Don't miss the beauty of this blessing. When Boaz blessed Ruth, he described her as coming under the wings of God for refuge. Tuck this picture in your mind, because we'll see it again shortly.

Under God's Wings of Refuge

Through Boaz's blessing, God was divinely arranging the details of Ruth's future. But God wasn't the only one. Naomi had a few ideas of her own. Wheels turning, Naomi saw the potential of Ruth and Boaz's relationship, and she cooked up *quite* the plan.

Naomi told Ruth to "wash, put on perfume, and get dressed in your best clothes. Then go down to the threshing floor. . . . When he [Boaz] lies down, note the place where he is lying. Then go and uncover his feet and lie down. He will tell you what to do" (3:3–4 NIV).

You might think this is the part of the story where we'd ask our kids to leave the room. Not to worry. In this culture, uncovering feet was a ceremonial, nonsexual act. It was a customary expression of how a woman showed submission. Ruth uncovered Boaz's feet as a symbol of her submission and willingness to become Boaz's wife.³ How's that for different?

That night, Ruth followed Naomi's advice. When Boaz awoke and found Ruth at his feet, she said, "I am Ruth, your servant. *Spread your wings* over your servant, for you are a redeemer" (v. 9).

"Spread your wings." I don't want you to miss the significance of this tender moment. When Boaz first met Ruth, he described her as coming under *God's wings* for refuge. Here, Ruth acknowledged Boaz as the one whose wings she was coming under—the place she would find refuge. Through this moving exchange, Boaz became the expression of God's love and provision for Ruth. He was the very fulfillment of the blessing he had spoken over Ruth's life.

Isn't this how God often works in times of grief or need? We may walk the lonely and dark road of loss and isolation. But that weight of grief lightens when God brings people into our life to be an expression of his love. Just as Ruth experienced God's wings of refuge through Boaz, we can experience God's wings of refuge through the lives of others.

An Honest Question

Years ago my best friend from childhood, Kellie, experienced something every mother fears—her child battling an incurable illness. Hannah's illness was unlike our emergency trip to the hospital with Charity. Rather than walking out of the hospital after a brief stay, Hannah and her family endured years of long, traumatic hospital stays and surgeries. Fighting to her last breath, precious Hannah passed from this life to the arms of her heavenly Father after a lifelong illness of eighteen years.

The heartbreak Kellie and her family have endured since losing Hannah has been agonizing and paralyzing. They continue to grieve the loss and cling to God's goodness, sovereignty, and love.

Close to Hannah's passing, one of Kellie's friends asked her an insensitive yet honest question: "Where's your God now?"

Though this question would have reduced me to tears, Kellie clung to God's goodness, which gave her the grace to respond in a way that revealed God's heart. "Where's God?" Kellie responded. "Where he's always been—in the hearts of his people, expressing his love to my family in our deepest pain."[4]

What kept Kellie walking through the unimaginable pain of losing her daughter was God's love flowing to her through others. Though God is not far from the brokenhearted, his nearness is often expressed through the love of others.

If you are currently in a challenging time, can you think of a friend who could help carry you through this season? A friend or community God could use as a place of refuge under his wings? Or perhaps God could use you to extend his love to others. We can easily be consumed by our own problems, but deep joy comes as we notice the needs of others and become an expression of God's love in their lives.

The Blessing

What began as a desperate situation for Ruth became a divine encounter, leading her to meet her husband and kinsman-redeemer. Not only that, with Ruth's redemption also came an unexpected blessing—a son.

Immediately after the birth of this son, the text shifts away from Ruth and Boaz and focuses on Naomi and the women rejoicing over this blessing. "The women living there said, 'Naomi has a son!'" (4:17 NIV).

I love this. The women recognized Ruth's baby as *Naomi's* son, underscoring how the book of Ruth is a story of hope—redeeming what was lost.

What do I mean? Naomi was no longer Mara. Her heart was transformed from bitter to pleasant. Though she had lost her biological sons, she gained a son-in-law, a grandson, and a daughter-in-law who was better to her than seven sons (v. 15).

> ## His nearness is often expressed through the love of others.

Sometimes we lose things in life that can never be replaced, but God blesses us with unexpected joys that refresh our hearts. The ache may linger, but as Jesus followers we are promised a place of perfect restoration after this life is over. A place where God will wipe every tear from our eyes, a place where death, mourning, crying, and pain will be no more (Rev. 21:4).

Despite loss and heartbreak, we are never forsaken by God. Because he is both righteous and just, he will redeem what was lost and, in his perfect time, make every wrong right. Every tear, every sleepless night, and every moment of despair will one day be overshadowed by his redeeming love and redemptive acts.

Truth and Trust

Boaz was a redeemer to Ruth and Naomi, a picture of who Jesus is to us. Just as Boaz spread his wings and paid the price to redeem Ruth, Jesus covers us and paid the price to save and redeem us. Our brokenness, barrenness, and sin are exchanged for his purpose, life, and forgiveness.

The book of Ruth gives us a glimpse into the gracious heart of God and his faithfulness to those who follow him. We see the exchanges of

> bitter for pleasant,
> widowed for married,
> barren for fruitful,
> foreigner for a daughter of God,
> desperate for resting under the wings of God.

What's more, the story of Ruth began with three deaths, but it ends with the birth of a son and a significant genealogy. Ruth's son was the father of Jesse, the father of King David (4:17). As our study continues, we'll see that David's descendants include the Seed—Jesus—who would redeem the world!

Think of this. Ruth, a pagan girl from a pagan country, through her selfless act, became a blessing to Naomi and was included in the line of the One who would bless the world.

> May we walk as an extension of his love,
> find refuge under his wings, and
> rejoice in our redemption through Jesus—our kinsman-redeemer.

Questions

Ruth's selfless decision changed Naomi's life. We never know the impact of our decision to love others—kids, spouse, relatives, neighbors, or those in need. What decisions or sacrifices are you making now, or could start making, that might affect someone else's future?

In what ways can you relate to Naomi's struggles?

When you walk through hard situations, do you ever let them define you?

Can you think of a time God brought you through a desperate situation? How did the situation change you?

How can the story of Naomi and Ruth help you perceive your problems differently?

JESSE TREE

What is something you want to remember about Ruth and Naomi?

TRACING
HIS
Hope
THROUGH
KINGS

Day 12

DAVID:
WHEN LIFE TAKES A TURN

Read 2 Samuel 7.

"David and Goliath" was my son's favorite bedtime Bible story, hands down. Every night that Isaiah requested it, I was confident he dreamed of one day being used just like David. But one night, after Ryan read Isaiah the story, I learned otherwise:

> Ryan: What did we learn about God from the story of David and Goliath?
> Isaiah: Dad, we learned God wants us to throw rocks at mean people!

Trying not to explode in laughter, Ryan listened to Isaiah's four-year-old logic. Then Ryan shared a bit of his own.

TRACING HIS HOPE THROUGH KINGS

While David is best known for his battle with Goliath, there's another story that carries an even greater significance, not only for David's life but also for the Old Testament narrative and the promise of Christ. That story is God's promise to David in 2 Samuel 7, which is where we begin today.

The scene opens in the palace of David, king of Israel. In this season of his life, David had conquered his surrounding enemies, and God had given him rest. During this time, David "summoned Nathan the prophet. 'Look,' David said, 'I am living in a beautiful cedar palace, but the Ark of God is out there in a tent!'" (2 Sam. 7:2 NLT).

Having recently relocated the ark of the covenant to Jerusalem, David was not content to gaze out his palace window and see the ark—the place of God's presence—sitting in the tent he had pitched for it. David dreamed of building a glorious temple for the ark.

At first Nathan encouraged David to follow his dream. David was, after all, Israel's anointed king and a man after God's heart (1 Sam. 13:14).

However, that night God spoke to Nathan with surprising news: David was not to build a house of worship.

Had Nathan misheard? Anyone could look at David's life and see he was the perfect candidate. He was the king of Israel. He deeply desired to build the temple and had, in fact, already made plans for it (1 Chron. 28:2). It didn't add up.

And yet isn't this a picture of how God often works? He sees things from a different perspective. He looks through a different lens. What we may perceive as a good idea—or even a great idea—may not be God's plan.

A Good Idea Versus God's Idea

Ryan and I experienced this disconnect between a good idea and God's plan when we believed God was leading us to plant a church in Arizona. After months of praying and planning, we packed the Penske moving van and ventured two thousand miles to follow our dream.

Everything fell into place once we arrived. We found great schools, fun friends, and a church eager to partner with us in the plant. Our anticipation of God's blessing could not have been greater.

Before starting the church, the launching church asked us to attend a church planters' assessment in Kansas City, Missouri. We packed our bags and made the trip, clicking our heels in anticipation—finish line in view.

But at the assessment, everything changed. On the last night, two leaders escorted us into a private room and shared the heartbreaking news: "Mr. and Mrs. Amidon, you are not approved to start a church."

TRACING HIS HOPE THROUGH KINGS

Our hearts shattered. Certainly, there was a mistake. Had they confused us with someone else? Didn't they know our hearts? Our passion? Our sacrifice? Planting a church was what we believed God had gifted us to do. It added up to an answer that did not make sense.

More than that, it hurt. God's plan was not our plan.

Perhaps this is your story. You had dreams and desires, only to realize God had other plans. Whether it's your career, family, marriage, ministry, education, or dream, life often turns out differently than we expect.

For many of us, the desire resides deep in our hearts. We made plans and sacrifices. But in the end, our plan was not God's plan. And sometimes it hurts.

Other factors can also be at play. Sometimes our dreams don't happen because of others' mistakes. Sometimes it's the fruit of our poor choices or the forces of evil. How these things intermingle with God's sovereignty is beyond today's discussion. For now, what's important is acknowledging that God is sovereign and allowed these things to happen.

Still, when disappointment comes, it's easy to get discouraged. Our unmet hopes can steer us away from God. Cynicism, depression, and anger can take root in our hearts. Or we become entangled in the web of regrets and endless what-ifs.

But know this, my friend: God has a better way. We can have hope.

I'm comforted that men and women in the Bible faced disappointments and detours. Their stories remind us that even when we feel like we're against a wall or forgotten by God, he is there with his master plan in place.

Day 12 | David: When Life Takes a Turn

This is the encouragement we will find through the life of King David and his place in the story of the coming Savior.

The Promise

I imagine when David first heard God's no, it came as a shock. But from heaven's perspective, God had his blueprint in place, marking out a course that David would have never dreamed.

God told David, "I will raise up your offspring after you, . . . and I will establish his kingdom. He shall build a house for my name, and I will establish the throne of his kingdom forever" (2 Sam. 7:12–13).

Forever. This is key.

Though David wanted to build a house for God, God wanted to build a house, or lineage, through David. Not only a lineage but an eternal throne and kingdom.

This was no small moment. Though David's son Solomon eventually built a physical temple, God promised David a descendant who would have a house, throne, and kingdom that would last forever. I would imagine you can guess who this descendant would be. Through David, the Messiah would come![1]

David wouldn't use smooth stones and a sling to kill another Goliath, nor would he build a physical house of worship. Instead, God promised to use David's life and legacy as the foundation on which Jesus would come. This promise is called the Davidic covenant—a covenant that builds upon the promises and covenants we have learned through our study:

- In the garden, God promised Adam and Eve a Redeemer (Gen. 3:15).

- Then, God promised Abraham that the Messiah would come from his descendants—the Hebrew people (Gen. 12; 15).
- God reiterated the promise of the Messiah coming through the family of Issac, Jacob, and Judah (Gen. 26:3–4; 28:14–15; 49:10).

Here with David, God narrowed the scope, and we learn that the Messiah would come from David's family. The eternal, all-knowing, all-loving God had his divine plan in place.

The New Testament Connection

Before we see David's response, I want us to delve deeper and watch how God's promise to David weaves into the bigger story of Jesus. You'll love this.

We begin with the first verse of the New Testament: "The book of the genealogy of Jesus Christ, the son of David, the son of Abraham" (Matt. 1:1).

I marvel at how the verse hinging the Old and New Testaments introduces Jesus as the fulfillment of God's promises to Abraham and David—promises stretching back over a thousand years.

The connections continue. When Gabriel appeared to Mary, he said Jesus "will be great and will be called the Son of the Most High. And the Lord God will give to him the *throne of his father David*, and he will reign over the house of Jacob forever, and of his kingdom there will be no end" (Luke 1:32–33).

Catch how this prophecy masterfully echoes God's promise to David. Jesus will have the throne of "his father David," where he will "reign . . . forever" over a kingdom that has "no end."

That's not all. As Jesus's earthly ministry unfolded, people called him the Son of David (Matt. 9:27; 15:22). The Jews knew the Messiah would come from David's descendants,[2] so the name "Son of David" speaks of more than genealogy. It was a messianic title, recognizing Jesus was the promised one of the Old Testament.

From the Gospels, we jump to the final book of the Bible—Revelation. Jesus said, "I am the root and the descendant of David" (22:16).

Consider this profound truth: Jesus is not only a *descendant* of David but is also the *root* of David. That is, Jesus came *before* David. He is before all things (Col. 1:17).

From Matthew to Revelation, Jesus is the one who fulfills the promise from generations before. Who can reasonably doubt these bookends are by design, crafted by our Creator?[3] Jesus—the Creator, the eternal God. From the beginning. Present all along.

David's Response

When God says no to our desires, it's not usually a comfortable place. David's story offers us a profound and practical lesson in responding to God. After hearing Nathan's prophecy, "David went in and sat before the LORD" (2 Sam. 7:18). David may have sat in the luxury of his palace or in the tattered tent where the ark of the covenant dwelled. Still, he sat. He reflected and prayed. Intimately. Personally.

Scripture tells us he recounted God's faithfulness and peered forward to what God had promised to do. In the end, David's heart was settled through worship and reflection on God's greatness and bigger plan.

There's power when we sit before the Lord. It's a place of stillness, uncluttered with the distraction of to-do lists or social media scrolls. It's a refuge of deep communion and transparency before God.

May I ask you a tender question? If you were to sit before God, what would you say? What if you took your unmet dreams and released them to his sovereign care?

> There's power when we sit before the Lord. It's a refuge of deep communion and transparency before God.

God's presence is a place of healing. It's where "he heals the broken-hearted and binds up their wounds" (Ps. 147:3). In his presence we remind ourselves that everything he does is first filtered through fingers of love. It's where we can take time to extend grace to ourselves for the regrets we carry.

In his presence we can release our tight grip of control and hold our dreams in open palms of surrendered trust. We can bend our knee to his sovereign plan and, at the same time, pour out our hearts to him, asking him to move in the way only he can.

I treasure the example we see in David. God redirected his life with a promise David would never see or fully know in his earthly life. Still, David responded in thankfulness, deep worship, and trust.

Humble Submission and Simple Trust

When Ryan and I received the news about the church plant, our hearts broke. Our bright, shiny dream became a confusing and surprising *no* from God. Though our plan was in pieces, we clung to what we knew was true: God loved us, he was with us, and he had a plan. Even though our plan was not his plan, we had to trust he knew what was best.

Seven years later, I look back on that season and am so thankful for God's deep work of transformation and knowing him more. The eager couple that traveled to Arizona was very different from the one that returned months later. We had moved to Arizona, confident we would build a thriving church and bring many to Jesus. Eight months later when we left Arizona and headed for the East Coast, our posture had changed. We were humbled. Surrendered.

Broken by life, yet held by God.

Ryan and I wanted to build a house for God, but there was something greater God wanted to build in us: humble submission and simple trust.

Truth and Trust

Despite the unexpected turn in David's life, God was there and had never left. He had been working the whole time, scripting a plan that exceeded David's expectations.

May we trust God's plan in our own lives. Even when situations don't make sense or the problem seems insurmountable. Even in heartbreaking disappointment, we can find peace, purpose, and calling in God's love and bigger plan.

What about you? What is the desire of your heart? Do you have a direction or dream you long to be fulfilled? What if today, rather than hold a tight grip over the situation, you cradled your desires with open hands of trust and surrender?

If you have disappointments, could you take time to simply sit—as David did—in the presence of the Lord, free from distraction? And there, in surrendered trust, come to him with your deepest desires.

Rest in this today: your heavenly Father is orchestrating every detail of your life.

He will complete the good work he began in you.
He loves you.
You don't need to be anxious, sit in self-pity, fear the future, or question his love.
His ways are perfect.
His love for you will never fail.

Questions

In this season of life, is there something you were set on happening a certain way, but it is different than you expected? Family? Career? Pregnancy? A relationship? School?

Think of that situation. What would happen if you released a tight grip, prayed for God to show himself strong, and held the outcome with open hands?

Can you think of an unexpected turn in your life that ended up being something better than you anticipated?

How does seeing God's faithfulness to fulfill his promises give you hope for what you face?

JESSE TREE

What is something you want to remember about the Davidic covenant?

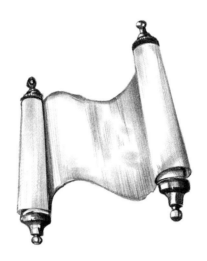

Day 13

JOSIAH:
LIFE IN DRY SEASONS

Read 2 Kings 22.

In the entryway of our local library is a used-book section. I remember when the library first set it up. It was full of books, well organized, and staffed with a library volunteer who was chatty and eager to help.

Happy for adult conversation, I let the kids loose in the library one day while I visited with the volunteer and browsed the books. As our conversation was ending, I asked the volunteer where I could find the Christian book section.

She paused, tilted her head like a puppy, and asked, "Christian books? Religion?"

"Yes. Christianity. Religion. You know, the life of Jesus."

"You mean the self-help section?"

"No." I chuckled awkwardly. "Not self-help. Books about God."

"I'm sorry," she replied. "We don't have a section like that. You may find something in the self-help section. Check there."

The library volunteer then escorted me through the maze of bookshelves to a yellow sign marked Self-Help. There, I found Christian books and copies of the Bible.

I was shocked.

Our culture has lost its reverence for the Bible, hasn't it? What was once honored as God's Word is now overlooked by most and mocked by many. And I've found that if we're not careful—actively guarding against culture's trends and the Enemy's lies—we, too, can forget the power of God's Word and miss the blessing of its liberating truth. We'll unknowingly feast on friendship with the world and live without God's power and peace.

If you're feeling a little worn by the pace of life, if you lack peace, need wisdom, or long for freshness in your relationship with God, lean in as we find encouragement through one of Judah's most memorable kings and forerunners of Jesus—King Josiah. Together we'll see how Josiah's shift toward God's Word reset the trajectory of his life and propelled the nation to spiritual revival.

A revival we can know as well.

Young Josiah Becomes King

King Josiah reigned several hundred years after the time of King David. David's son Solomon had constructed the temple. Soaring over forty feet high, the temple reflected the people's devotion to and worship of God.[1]

However, this high regard for God and the temple was short-lived. After Solomon's death, Israel divided into two nations: Israel in the north and Judah in the south. When the Northern Kingdom persisted in idolatry, God removed his hand of protection. As a result, they fell to the Assyrians.

The Southern Kingdom of Judah remained but struggled with its own idolatry. When a king named Manasseh, Josiah's grandfather, came to power, things went from bad to worse. King Manasseh built altars to pagan deities and practiced sorcery, divination, and witchcraft. He even sacrificed his own sons. The worst part? Much of this was done in the temple—the holy place of God's presence (2 Kings 21:2–7). Though Manasseh repented toward the end of his life, the idolatry he instilled persisted among the people.

The Southern Kingdom took another moral nosedive when Manasseh's son Amon became king. Amon ruled for just two years before his servants murdered him.

Then entered Josiah, who inherited the throne.

Day 13 | Josiah: Life in Dry Seasons

Imagine what Josiah faced. He assumed his position as king with zero spiritual heritage, and the nation swarmed with idolatry. The temple of God was the center of unthinkable acts, and Judah faced inevitable annihilation.

If that wasn't enough, Josiah became king at only eight years old. I don't know how many eight-year-old boys you've talked to lately, but from a human perspective, the situation seemed grim.

But isn't this the brilliant way God works? God views the world through a different lens. He doesn't judge by outward appearance. When God's eyes locked on Josiah, he saw a young boy with a passion and zeal fit for leading a nation to revival.

The Discovery

Ten years into his reign, Josiah began a project to restore the temple. What started as a campaign to upgrade the physical building became a spiritual revival through one incredible discovery—the book of the law. This book was most likely the first five books of our Old Testament.[2]

This was not just an extra Bible lying around the temple or something tucked away in the self-help section. The high priest Hilkiah "found" the book of the law, implying that it had been lost (2 Kings 22:8). Not only had the book been lost, it had been ignored and forgotten.

You would think finding such a treasure would have prompted celebration—maybe a hallelujah and a happy dance or a selfie with the scroll. But when Josiah heard the Law's contents, he reacted very differently. He tore his clothes in great distress because he realized the extent to which Judah had deviated from God's holy standard.

More than that, King Josiah would have heard the conditions God set forth in the Mosaic covenant: blessings for obedience and punishment for disobedience. Aware of Judah's rebellious state, King Josiah knew judgment was inevitable. Yet this young king, broken by the people's rebellion, would use God's Word to bring his people back to God.

Orange Tree in the Desert

Have you ever noticed there's a temptation in every season of life to think we'll have more time for God's Word in the next? When we're in school, we think we'll have more time after we graduate. When we're single, we're convinced we'll have more time when we get married. When our kids are young, we think things will be easier once they're older. And on it goes.

This was my mindset in my early years of marriage—before we had children. Life felt beyond hectic, and I could not *wait* to have kids so life would finally slow down and I'd have more time in my day.

We can all burst into laughter now.

Boy, was I in for a surprise. Caring for a real baby was nothing like playing with Cabbage Patch Kids as a little girl. I went from working full time to staying home with a fussy baby and wondering what had happened to my life.

I needed help. Not self-help. Holy Spirit help.

At the time, we lived in Arizona, where our house backed up to the desert. Though our large backyard of rocks and cacti required little work, there was one large orange tree that needed water almost daily.

One morning while Charity was napping, I glanced out the large bay window, and my eyes locked on the orange tree. It didn't look the same. The once lush tree was worn and dull. The leaves were shriveled and faded. Fruit was sparse.

I felt as if I was staring at my own reflection—worn and dull, desperate for life and lacking fruit. I thought, *Father, I want to thrive in this season, and I know it comes from being in your presence and in your Word.*

Then the simple thought hit me: *The tree needs water, and I need time with God. I'll do both!* I walked to the back porch and turned on the hose to water the tree. Then I went into the living room, sat in the bay window, and spent time in prayer and the Word—orange tree in view. When I finished, I turned off the water.

This became my habit. The more I spent time with God, the more water the tree received. And no surprise, life occurred in both the tree and me.

Of course, things competed for my time with God, and both the tree and I would suffer (not to mention my dear husband). But one quick look at the tree motivated me to return to God's Word.

As odd as it sounds, that orange tree became a treasured image of the life and joy God's Word brought to my heart during those early years of motherhood. It was spiritual revival, and it all began with God's Word.

Spiritual Revival

King Josiah's passion for the book of the law not only moved him emotionally, it moved him to action. He led Judah in reform, beginning with the people hearing the book of the law and recommitting to the covenant to follow the Lord and keep his commandments.

After this renewed commitment, Josiah went through the temple and surrounding regions, eliminating idolatry. He destroyed the altars and high places where people worshiped idols. He defiled the locations of child sacrifices. He tore down the living quarters of the male prostitutes in the temple. Finally, Josiah reinstated the Passover, which had not been celebrated "like that since the time when the judges ruled in Israel, nor throughout all the years of the kings of Israel and Judah" (2 Kings 23:22 NLT).

Connection to Christ

Many of us may know of Josiah's young age when he became king, but there's a detail of his life that may be less familiar. Three hundred years *before* Josiah's birth, an unnamed prophet spoke to an altar in the town of Bethel and said, "O altar, altar, thus says the LORD: 'Behold, a son shall be born to the house of David, Josiah by name, and he shall sacrifice on you [this altar] the priests of the high places who make offerings on you, and human bones shall be burned on you'" (1 Kings 13:2).

What an unusual prophecy. The prophet spoke *to* the altar, telling it that one day a man named Josiah would burn ungodly priests' bones on it. Catch this profound connection. During Josiah's reform, Josiah traveled to Bethel, removed illegitimate priests' bones from the graves, and burned the bones on the exact altar the prophet spoke to three hundred years earlier (2 Kings 23:15–16).

As an interesting side note, King Josiah is one of only a handful of people in the Bible whose life, accomplishments, and name were prophesied long *before* their births. His commitment to God's Word made a mark in history, and his life and leadership stand out as some of the most significant in the Bible.

And in this prophecy to the altar, did you notice that Josiah was born to the house of David? King Josiah was both a descendant of David and in the lineage of Jesus Christ (Matt. 1:11).

Truth and Trust

Today we have seen a man who caught the eye of God. Scripture summarizes his life by saying: "Neither before nor after Josiah was there a king like him who turned to the LORD as he did—with all his heart and with all his soul and with all his strength" (2 Kings 23:25 NIV).

Josiah is not remembered for his charisma, charm, talent, looks, or popularity. Rather, he turned to God and obeyed his Word. This reminds me of Peter's encouragement: "Like newborn babies, you must crave pure spiritual milk so that you will grow into a full experience of salvation. Cry out for this nourishment" (1 Peter 2:2 NLT).

Peter pleaded with his reader. "Crave and cry out for God's Word. Let it nourish you." When we do, we can enjoy the full experience of salvation. Not just a Sunday occurrence or enough to get by. But life overflowing.

When we refuse to drink from the world's empty wells and drink from God's Word, change happens. Like the orange tree in the desert, wilted leaves come alive and dullness turns to vibrancy. Barrenness turns to fruit. The Word encourages, transforms, corrects, and liberates. It makes me the wife I long to be, the mom my kids need me to be, and the friend this world needs me to be.

My desire and prayer for you is that today's study plants a seed that produces the fruit of spending time in God's Word.

Be nourished by it.
Walk in the fullness and fruit of knowing God.
Not through self-help but by a Holy Spirit–empowered
life.

Questions

Wherever you are in your journey of knowing God, I want you to be encouraged by how the Bible personally affects our lives. God's Word:

- renews my mind;
- brings peace to my racing thoughts;
- centers me on Christ;
- reminds me to live for an audience of One;
- helps me know God;
- brings comfort in times of grief;
- brings encouragement and hope in times of despair;
- shows me the way to eternal life;
- brings correction;
- gives wisdom and the right perspective on life;

- gives a sense of purpose; and
- inspires me to worship God.

From the list above, mark two or three that you have especially seen in your own life. Explain.

Are there any things you could add to the above list?

Romans 12:2 says, "Do not be conformed to this world, but be transformed by the renewal of your mind." Why is it so important to renew your mind through his Word?

Josiah turned to God and obeyed his Word. When we turn to God, it implies we may be turning away from something else. What things come in your life as hindrances to walking with God or spending time with him?

The orange tree was a picture of my time with God. Is there something you could use around your house to represent your time with God or remind you to spend time with him?

JESSE TREE

What is something you want to remember about Josiah?

Day 14

JESSE TREE:
YOUR STORY ISN'T OVER

Read Isaiah 11:1–9.

When Ryan and I were in student ministry, we packed two buses full of teenagers and traveled to a weeklong camp. The first morning, the students poured into the conference room buzzing with hundreds of other students from the area.

After a time of worship, the speaker shared a compelling message about believing lies about ourselves. "Maybe you feel useless or that your life was a mistake. You might feel like you're not important or not talented. It's a lie! You're living by a label."

As the message concluded, each student received a blank name tag on which they wrote the lie they were living. A hush swept across the room. Once finished, they dropped their name tags in baskets and left.

When Ryan and I grabbed our belongings to leave, the speaker motioned us and other leaders to a side room to review the name tags. We circled the table and the speaker spread out the name tags. The dimly lit room fell silent as we witnessed what our eyes could not believe. Of the hundreds of name tags, one word saturated the stack. What was so chilling was that this word was not limited to a specific age, grade, church, or section of the room.

The word? *Invisible.* The students felt invisible.

The speaker scanned our faces, lowered his voice, and said, "Do you know what strikes me? I never suggested the word *invisible* in my message. I didn't even say it. This is the whisper of the Enemy himself!"

He was right. Yet as certain as we were about the Enemy's work, we were also confident in something greater: God saw the students differently. They may have felt invisible, but their lives were not hidden from God.

This story reminds me that when man sees one thing, God sees something different. When we feel one way, the reality from God's perspective may differ.

That's where today's study comes in.

So far in our journey, we have learned about God through story—or historical narrative. Today we shift to prophecy and get a glimpse into God's perspective and plan for his people and their future.

Day 14 | Jesse Tree: Your Story Isn't Over

Today and for the next three days, we'll look at incredible prophesies from Isaiah, who foretold of Christ's coming more than any other prophet. I'm excited about today's prophecy because it is the basis for the Jesse Tree tradition you can begin with your family, using what we've learned through our time together. (See the appendixes for more.)

Prophecy of a Branch

When Ryan and I moved from Arizona to North Carolina, to say our yard was overgrown would have been an understatement. As young homeowners who had only cared for cacti, rocks, and a beloved orange tree, we were overwhelmed.

Two massive trees in our front yard blocked the view of the house from the road. Our first project involved paying landscapers a small fortune to remove them. Once the trees were gone, only bare stumps remained. The difference was unbelievable.

How does this connect to today's prophecy? Under King David's leadership, Israel had been like a towering tree in the height of a North Carolina spring—powerful, majestic, and fruitful. But because of sin and idolatry, the nation had split into two warring nations—Israel and Judah—and God was removing his hand of protection. As a result, the once towering and fruitful nation would be like a massive tree cut to a bare stump. From a human perspective, their story was over. Their name tag would have read *dead* or *lifeless*.

But God had a different perspective.

> *There shall come forth a shoot from the stump of Jesse,*
> *and a branch from his roots shall bear fruit.*
> *(Isa. 11:1)*

175

TRACING HIS HOPE THROUGH KINGS

Though Judah's future appeared bleak, God saw something different.[1] Life would come! Judah's story was not over.

Isaiah's prophecy of a coming branch is even more compelling because Judah was not the only nation that would be cut down. In chapter 10, Isaiah said Assyria—an enemy nation—would be like a forest of trees cut down like a stump.[2]

Picture the message Isaiah is conveying. A dense forest of towering trees reduced to lifeless stumps. All the stumps would remain dead or dormant except one. One stump would stand in stark contrast to the others. The stump from Jesse, and only Jesse, would produce a branch.

This wouldn't be any branch. The brilliance of Isaiah's prophecy is *who* the branch represents: "And the Spirit of the LORD shall rest upon him" (v. 2). "Upon him"—the branch is a *person* who would come from the stump of Jesse.

Let me put this together. If you remember from our study on Ruth (day 11), Jesse was the father of King David. The branch from the stump of Jesse would be a descendant of Jesse, King David's father.

Is this sounding familiar? Today's prophecy reaffirms God's promise to David from three hundred years earlier—the Davidic covenant: the promise that a King with an eternal throne would come through the lineage of David (day 12, 2 Sam. 7).

Though Judah may have felt this was the end, God had a different perspective. The stump of Jesse sprouted the Seed who would bring hope to the world!

Isaiah continues with a description of this person:

Day 14 | Jesse Tree: Your Story Isn't Over

And the Spirit of the LORD shall rest upon him,
the Spirit of wisdom and understanding,
the Spirit of counsel and might,
the Spirit of knowledge and the fear of the LORD.
And his delight shall be in the fear of the LORD.

(11:2–3)

From the barren nation and its line of kings, a descendant of Jesse would spring forth like a fresh branch from a dead stump. Think of how refreshing Isaiah's prophecy would have been. The Branch would delight in the fear of the Lord. He would be unlike the godless kings that Israel and Judah had known for generations.

Isaiah said the Spirit of the Lord would *rest* on him. The Spirit would not come and go as he did with the other men and women of the Old Testament. Jesus would experience something different. The Spirit of the Lord would rest and remain on him. What's more? In these few verses, we see evidence of all three persons of the Trinity: Father (Lord), Son (Branch), and Spirit.[3]

This branch would be Jesus—God in the flesh, full of the Spirit, bringing hope to the world.

Behind the Scenes

One December afternoon a few years ago, I went to *The Nutcracker* ballet with friends. Following the finale and eruption of applause, we rose to leave. Suddenly, light covered the stage, the orchestra struck up a melody, and the curtain lifted to reveal dancers in new costumes performing a final piece. It was breathtaking.

I've experienced moments like this before, but that afternoon was different. An unusual peace came over me. As I sat in my chair, overwhelmed by the wonder and beauty of that unexpected moment, I thought, *Isn't this just like our heavenly Father? Isn't this what he does?*

We may think our story is over. We may feel as if the curtain is down or only a dead stump remains. We may think our name tag says *forgotten*. Little do we know that just as the dancers, musicians, and stage crew were behind the curtain preparing for the unexpected performance, the hidden hand of God is working in ways we cannot see.

Truth and Trust

When I consider Isaiah's prophecy, I think of times when I have felt cut down to a stump. Dead. My story was over. The name tag read *defeated*. Yet Isaiah's words remind me that God has a perspective I do not have. Dead stumps do not mean dead ends. When we see a barren stump, God sees an opportunity for new life.

Do you ever feel like your story is over? Or cut down to a stump? Is there an area of your life that needs a fresh filling of God's Spirit? Have you ever considered that God sees your situation differently?

Hold to this truth today: God can breathe life into the deadness of a marriage. He can give direction for a derailed career, spur conviction in a rebellious child, and provide healing for hurt. He takes the dead things of our life and redeems them for his glory.

> Dead stumps do not mean dead ends. When we see a barren stump, God sees an opportunity for new life.

Day 14 | Jesse Tree: Your Story Isn't Over

Despite the situation in your life that seems impossible, the news you just heard that feels hopeless, or the dead stump that looks like a dead end, know that God has not finished writing his story. We don't need to run from him or resist his presence. Rather, you and I can come, confident that as we draw close to him, he will draw close to us (James 4:8). In his presence, we ask him to do what only he can do:

Breathe life into the lifeless.
Speak truth to our heart.
Bring hope to what seems lost.

Despite the seeming end of Judah, God promised life through a tender shoot—hope for God's people then, hope for you and me now.

His name is Jesus!

Questions
***

How does the prophecy of the Branch show God's faithfulness to a faithless people?

Is there some part of your life that feels as if it has been reduced to a stump?

In the situation you just mentioned, what is your hope and prayer?

What, if any, evidence do you see of God working behind the scenes in your situation? Do you see hints of hope or new life?

How can the prophecy of the Branch bring hope to you or someone you love?

JESSE TREE

What is something you want to remember about the Branch?

TRACING
HIS
Peace
THROUGH
PROPHECY

Day 15

HE IS OUR PEACE

Read Isaiah 26:3; Philippians 4:6–7.

When I was a little girl, I always loved when my dad asked me to join him on one of his flights. Even though I could barely see over the instrument panel, he would let me sit in the copilot's chair and "help" him fly the small plane. I savored the sensation of swimming through the clouds and feeling like I could touch the sun.

One flight did not carry the same joy. Just outside Cincinnati, our plane plowed through a severe storm. The rain pounded the windshield like rounds of ammunition, and we bounced like a marionette on a string.

Dad didn't seem bothered by the storm—at all. But my nine-year-old mind was in a panic, certain of disaster. At the height of the noise and jostling, Dad's hand slowly reached to radio the control tower.

Oh no! I thought. *Will he tell them we're going down?* I couldn't bear to hear the news.

He picked up the radio. "N7167Y. Reporting moderate turbulence."

Was he kidding? *Moderate* turbulence? Were we on the same plane? I was sure our landing would not be at the airport but in eternity.

Have you ever noticed how two people can be in the same situation, but one is panicked and the other is at peace? One foresees a dreadful end, while the other calls things "bumpy"?

On the flight with Dad, I envisioned the worst and panicked. But Dad saw things differently. He knew the dangers of the storm, what our plane could handle, and how to keep us safe. Even though we endured turbulence, Dad knew the storm's strength would not overtake us. It was this perspective that gave him peace.

Today's study thrills me. Because if there's something we would all like to experience more, it's peace. We're stretched and pulled and feel the constant need to keep up. Many of us carry deep concerns for loved ones and worry for their future. And when the storms of life hit, our weary hearts are beaten by the turbulence of stress and uncertainty. Peace is often the exception, not the norm.

But Jesus—the Prince of Peace—invites us to know peace in this life and for the life to come. So take a deep breath, push pause on your day, and know the Spirit longs to do a beautiful work in your heart.

The Peace *of* God and Peace *with* God

Today, we study one of the most beloved prophecies of the coming Christ. Isaiah wrote:

> *For to us a child is born,*
> *to us a son is given;*
> *and the government shall be upon his shoulder,*
> *and his name shall be called*
> *Wonderful Counselor, Mighty God,*
> *Everlasting Father, Prince of Peace.*
>
> (9:6)

Isaiah's prophecy not only foretells of Christ's power and deity, but it also reveals how Jesus would satisfy the desire of every human heart. He would be the Wonderful Counselor, Mighty God, Everlasting Father, and Prince of Peace.

When we study peace in the Bible, we see two phrases used: peace *with* God and peace *of* God. Paul spoke of peace *with* God in Romans: "Since we have been justified by faith, we have peace with God through our Lord Jesus Christ" (5:1).

This is the type of peace that comes through our salvation—our right standing before God. When we put our faith in Jesus, we are no longer enemies of God or under his wrath (John 3:36; Rom. 5:10). We are forgiven, free, and in a right relationship with him. We have peace with God.

And yet if we're honest, even though we have peace with God, sometimes we do not feel peaceful. Life brings unrest. There's an inner angst, and we lack the peace God promises to all who follow him—a peace the Bible calls the peace *of* God.

Often the world describes peace as the absence of trouble: a smooth takeoff, flight, and landing. But biblical peace is not the absence of trouble. It's peace *despite* the trouble.

But is this even possible? Yes. Paul spoke of this type of peace—the peace of God—in Philippians. Before we look at his teaching, let's read the promise of peace from Jesus himself: "Peace I leave with you; my peace I give to you. Not as the world gives do I give to you" (John 14:27).

Jesus gave us peace—his peace. It's unlike what the world offers. It's supernatural, sourced in him alone.

But Jesus didn't stop there. He continued with instructions: "Let not your hearts be troubled, neither let them be afraid" (v. 27).

This is something we cannot miss. When Jesus promised peace, he gave us something to do. Jesus instructed us to actively guard against what comes so naturally to the human heart—worry and fear.

Many things detract from our sense of well-being. Wouldn't you agree? For example, lack of sleep, diet, exercise, life stage, workload, hormones (help us all), and even the weather affect our sense of peace. You may have your own list as well.

We won't take time to explore the complexities of our minds and bodies. Still, as we study Scripture, we find one practice that is a necessary means to walking in peace. It is the axis around which the peace of God revolves—prayer.

Day 15 | He Is Our Peace

This leads us to Paul's words about the peace of God in Philippians: "Do not be anxious about anything, but in everything by prayer and supplication with thanksgiving let your requests be made known to God. And the peace of God, which surpasses all understanding, will guard your hearts and your minds in Christ Jesus" (4:6–7).

Do you see the connection? It's as if Paul reaches back to Christ's words in John 14 and then continues with a Spirit-inspired plan for experiencing the peace of God.

Complaints Versus Requests

It is easy to read familiar passages like Philippians 4:6–7 and miss their truth. Sometimes when I'm not getting it, God uses unexpected and memorable ways to reveal just how transforming his Word can be.

When our kids were little, they went through a stage where they complained about everything. *Mom, I'm thirsty. Mom, I'm bored. Mom, I'm hungry.*

One afternoon, I'd had enough, so I told the kids things would change. I explained, "When you need something, don't complain. Ask nicely, and I'll be here to help."

It may sound radical, but from that day forward, apart from bleeding knees and emergencies, I would not answer their complaints. I'd simply ask them to turn their complaint into a request. After countless reminders, my children understood the difference between complaining and requesting. In time, complaints like "I'm hungry" and "I'm bored" became "May I have something to eat?" and "May I have a friend over to play?" It was a parental game changer.

Not long after my conversation with the kids, I felt like God tapped *me* on the shoulder and asked if I might think about doing the same thing with him. He's so good that way, isn't he? Rather than hearing my list of complaints, God wanted me to *ask* for what I needed, and he'd be there to help.

About that time I was reading Philippians 4: "Do not be anxious about anything . . ." (v. 6). However, this time I noticed something different. "Do not be anxious about anything, but . . . with thanksgiving, let your *requests* be made known to God."

Requests? Bring my requests? Had that always been there? I realized what I had been calling "prayer" was nothing more than me rehearsing a careful inventory of my complaints. Not much peace there. Just as I was telling my kids to ask me, God was calling me to ask him.

Couldn't we all grow in this area? I know I could. How often do our prayers sound like this:

> Dear God,
> It's been a rough week. I'm exhausted. This pace is
> driving me crazy. [Exhale] In Jesus's name. Amen.

Funny, isn't it? How much faith does it take to complain? What can God do with complaints? If God is pleased by our faith, how pleased is he by hearing our catalog of troubles?

Of course, there are times for lamenting and pouring out our burdens before God. Peter said to "cast all your anxiety on him because he cares for you" (1 Peter 5:7 NIV). But if we only march around the mountain of complaints, we never move to the path of peace.

Since my prayers had been mostly complaining, I knew it was time for a change. I grabbed my journal and listed all my concerns (a.k.a. *complaints*) down the left side of the paper. Then out from each concern, I wrote a short prayer of what I was asking God to do in that situation.

> ### If we only march around the mountain of complaints, we never move to the path of peace.

My complaint that *This pace is crazy* turned into *Father, give me wisdom to see where and why I'm overcommitting. Help me use my time well.*

My complaint that *I'm worried for the kids* became *Anoint me to teach my children about you. Let my life be an example, and keep their hearts tender toward you.*

Requests, not complaints. And then to end my prayer, *I confess my trust in you.*

Know this: when we are walking in the confidence of his provision, we are walking in peace. Every anxiety turns to prayer. Every fear turns to faith. Every worry is an opportunity to trust an unfailing God. Prayerful people are peaceful people.

Truth and Trust

As we end today, I want to look at one final encouragement from Proverbs 31. If you are familiar with this chapter, you may feel inspired—or like me, sometimes intimidated—by this godly woman. Still, we can learn from her life, especially how she views the future: "Strength and dignity are her clothing, and she laughs at the time to come" (v. 25). The New Living Translation says, "She laughs without fear of the future."

What joy! The Proverbs 31 woman is not wrenched with anxiety and fear, constantly rehearsing her concerns. She has joy and peace.

This joyful perspective is not ignorant bliss or wishful thinking. Nor is it living in denial or suppressing hurt, pain, or fear. Rather, it is confidence fixed on God and his good character. It belongs to someone who knows that neither life, nor death, nor things present nor things to come will be able to separate her from the love of God in Christ Jesus (Rom. 8:38–39).

This perspective provides perfect peace because our mind is set on Christ and we trust in him (Isa. 26:3). When anxieties come or when past pains feel like fresh wounds, we won't march around the mountain of complaints, but we move to the path of peace. We bring our requests to God, confident he will answer in his perfect way and time.

Do you long for this type of peace? How would it change the atmosphere of your home? How would it impact your relationships with your husband, children, friends, or roommate? How would it affect the way you interacted with your neighbors or colleagues? How would a sense of peace affect your well-being and emotions? Your habits, health, and sleep?

You *can* live a life of peace. It centers on knowing the Pilot—the Prince of Peace, the One who has control of the plane and the storm (Matt. 8:24–27). And when the Pilot says not to let your hearts be troubled or afraid, we can trust his words, experience his peace, and find rest for our souls.

He is the

Wonderful Counselor
Mighty God
Everlasting Father
Prince of Peace

Hallelujah!

Questions

Can you think of someone who exemplifies a life of peace? What makes them peaceful?

In the opening illustration of the plane in the storm, it was the pilot's perspective and control that brought peace. How can you apply this to an area of your life?

Paul said to bring our requests to God. Take a moment to list some recent or ongoing areas of stress and anxiety in your life. Then, beside each item on the list, write a request, asking God for what you want him to do.

How would your life be different if you started taking your requests rather than your complaints to God? Be specific.

JESSE TREE

What is something you want to remember about the Prince of Peace?

Day 16

HE IS MY SHEPHERD

Read Psalm 23; John 10:1–18.

A few summers ago, my kids were playing the laser-pointer game with a dog in our neighborhood. They'd race the little red dot down the sidewalk, amused by the dog's fun yet frantic attempts to capture the light. The dog would pounce on the dot, thinking he had caught his prey, only to realize he'd smacked the sidewalk. The kids would shine the light again, and off he'd go—eyes blazing for the prize.

TRACING HIS PEACE THROUGH PROPHECY

While watching the kids play, my neighbor surprised me by saying, "Did you know this game can be harmful to dogs?"

Taken aback by his comment, I asked him to explain. He said the light triggers the dog's predator instinct. But the problem is the dog never experiences the reward of the chase. The dog thinks he's captured the light but has grasped nothing. When the game ends, the dog is anxious and confused—continually searching for something he'll never find. It's an endless game of chase with no reward.

As we walked home that night, I thought, *Aren't we the same way?* Distracted by life's shiny laser lights. Drawn by desires we think will satisfy, only to realize they're an empty chase. We chase the "likes" of others, the promotion, the purchase, the better body, the luxury, or the substance—all while living under the illusion of satisfaction: *When I get what I want, I'll be satisfied.*

Perhaps your heart is set on a project at work. You are tiring yourself with late hours, and it's affecting your relationships. Perhaps you're chasing a certain appearance but never feel attractive enough. Maybe you experienced an unexpected setback in life and are constantly trying to catch up to where you think you should be. Perhaps you feel pressured to create a full life for your kids, but the nonstop pace is draining you.

I don't know about you, but I need guidance. I need correction when I head in the wrong direction and protection from pursuits that harm me. I need comfort in times of disappointment and confusion. I need to be led by something other than a laser light of distraction. I need someone who will take me by the hand and say *this* is the way—walk in it.

I need a shepherd, a good shepherd.

Day 16 | He Is My Shepherd

My guess is, you do too.

My Shepherd—and Yours

To this point in Israel's history, we have seen a nation whose sin and rebellion backed them into a corner of defeat. They'd chased laser lights of idol worship, false gods, and the world's ways. Beyond that, they had been ruled by a long list of leaders who had brought the nation to ruin (Ezek. 34).

Into this place of defeat, God spoke his word, promising to bring a new Shepherd. Someone to guide his people. Today's prophecy from Isaiah describes this Shepherd beautifully.

> *He tends his flock like a shepherd:*
> *He gathers the lambs in his arms*
> *and carries them close to his heart;*
> *he gently leads those that have young.*
> *(40:11 NIV)*

Do you sense the intimacy with which Isaiah wrote? The loving emotion his words convey. The coming Messiah would not be like the self-centered kings Israel had known. This Shepherd would tend and feed his flock. He would gather the lambs in his arms, carry them close to his heart, and gently lead them.

Sometimes we may picture God as distant or impersonal—someone barking orders and making threats. We may think of him as a toxic boss or disappointed parent. Yet Isaiah's words remind us of the tenderness of God's loving care and the intimacy he desires.

This comforting picture of a shepherd appears throughout the Scriptures, with the pinnacle passage being Psalm 23:

The LORD is my shepherd; I shall not want.
He makes me lie down in green pastures.
He leads me beside still waters.
He restores my soul.

(vv. 1–3)

Don't you love how David used the word *my*? The Lord was David's Shepherd. And he's yours too. *Personally.*

Consider the rich experience that inspired David's words. For years he had walked the hills of Bethlehem as a shepherd, tending the sheep. During those long days and nights, he wasn't scrolling his phone or texting his brothers on the battlefield. He was alone—with his Lord and with his sheep.

There, he learned the attention a good shepherd gives the flock. He experienced the extent to which a shepherd goes to protect the sheep. In the stillness of that season, David had perceived something of God's character that echoes into our hearts years later.

Everything the sheep needs, the shepherd has.

The Sheep Know His Voice

A few years ago, our homeschool group traveled to Pennsylvania and visited an Amish family's farm. After dinner, the owner asked if we would like to watch him gather the sheep for the night. Though we uttered a reserved yes, our hearts skipped with excitement.

The shepherd smiled, then took long strides up a grassy hill peppered with grazing sheep. Once up the hill and standing among the sheep, he spoke a quick command. Within seconds the sheep scurried toward him—some swiftly, others hobbling along. He spoke again, and the sheep followed him down the hill, crossed a small bridge, and found rest in another pasture.

The stillness and simple beauty of that moment overwhelmed us. The sheep knew his voice, and they followed him. The shepherd went before the flock, leading them in green pastures. Every action of the shepherd was for their protection, safety, and good. That night our eyes witnessed what our hearts needed to remember: we have a *Good* Shepherd.

Perhaps the reason we often run to other things—the reason we chase the laser lights of this world—is because we've forgotten or failed to see the goodness of God. We've forgotten that any other pursuit is an empty chase. While our soul may scramble for satisfaction and relief, the truth is that we have a Shepherd, and he has everything we need.

Jesus as the Good Shepherd

Seven hundred years after Isaiah prophesied of the gentle Shepherd, Jesus walked the hills of Galilee and gave seven different "I am" statements about himself and his ministry. In John 10, he announced, "The thief comes only to steal and kill and destroy. I came that they may have life and have it abundantly. *I am* the good shepherd. The good shepherd lays down his life for the sheep" (vv. 10–11).

What makes Jesus's statement so significant is the context in which he spoke it. Only moments before, he had healed a man blind from birth. But the Pharisees, rather than rejoice in the man's miracle, railed against Jesus and cast the man out of the temple.

Clearly, the Pharisees were not good shepherds. They weren't the evil kings of ancient Israel, but their intent was similar—selfish and opposed to God's plan. They were like the thieves coming to steal and destroy.

In response to their actions, Jesus revealed who he was: the *Good Shepherd*.

Do you think we ever face similar opposition? Of course, we don't have Pharisees condemning us or casting us out of the temple. But we may have church leaders who have misrepresented God's heart to us, wounding us by their words or actions. Our Enemy may flood our minds with negativity, doubt, and temptation. He cunningly works to distort God's goodness in our minds. Like the Pharisees, he longs to pull us away from Jesus and the flock.

Why? Because he knows if we doubt the goodness of the Shepherd, we'll run to other things.

But Jesus, the Good Shepherd, loves us and lays his life down for us. He rescues us from the destructive forces working against us. In him we find rest for our souls and satisfaction for the things we crave.

Truth and Trust

On a stretch of road by our home in North Carolina, there were two houses that shared a property line but could not have been more opposite in appearance. One was a luxurious estate set on a hill far from the road. It had a private, gated entry, pillared porch, multicar garage, swimming pool, and extensive stables. Next to the estate, not far from the road, was a small brick house on a modest lot.

When the kids were younger and we traveled this road, I would ask the same question every time we passed the two homes: "Which family do you think is happier? Who has more joy?"

Day 16 | He Is My Shepherd

Charity and Isaiah learned to anticipate my answer: "The outside doesn't matter. The family with Jesus has more joy." A lesson for them—and for me.

Gorgeous homes, luxury, entertainment, beauty, or success never satisfy our deepest desires. We may enjoy them, but looking to them for satisfaction is an empty chase—a laser light on the cement sidewalk.

As we close, I want to show you one of my favorite details about Jesus the Good Shepherd. Immediately before Jesus announced he was the Good Shepherd, he said, "I came that they may have life and have it abundantly" (John 10:10). Catch the powerful connection. Abundant life happens in the context of Jesus being our Shepherd. It has nothing to do with possession but with proximity to the Shepherd.

The power of abundant life is that we can be wiping dirty noses, making dinner, working, or enjoying the simple pleasures of life and still know abundance. When the Lord is my Shepherd, my eyes won't pine for more. I lack for nothing because I'm satisfied by the Good Shepherd.

> Abundant life happens in the context of Jesus being our Shepherd. It has nothing to do with possession but with proximity to the Shepherd.

Do you long for the abundant life Jesus offers but find yourself chasing other things? You have desires, but you're exhausted by the pursuit and you realize it's an empty chase.

I'm convinced one reason so many people are unhappy is because we think happiness comes from things. If we want to be happy sheep, we need to say no to the luring voices and yes to the Good Shepherd's plan.

I long for this, don't you? What if today you could go in a new direction? What if you could run to the One who leads you in paths of righteousness, the One who prepares a feast of his goodness even when evil surrounds you, the One who restores your soul (Ps. 23)?

And what if, when you're tempted to chase the laser light, you could pause and confess these simple words?

Lord, I come to you.
You have everything I need.
You satisfy my deepest desires.
You replace the Enemy's lies with truth.
You heal the wounding of my heart.
Tether me to truth and your plan.
I run to you.

Questions

Ask the Holy Spirit to identify areas in your life where he wants you to rest in his love rather than chase after things. What are these things?

In times of temptation, how can you run to God rather than chase the laser lights of distraction?

Describe a time when the Enemy wanted to distort the goodness of God in your mind.

How does knowing the Good Shepherd connect to living an abundant life?

JESSE TREE
What is something you want to remember about the Good Shepherd?

Day 17

HE WILL SUFFER FOR ME

Read Isaiah 53.

In the 1960s Barry Leventhal was the offensive captain of the UCLA football team. Having just led his team to the Rose Bowl championship, he was on top of the world.

A few weeks after the game, Barry was introduced to Hal—the Campus Crusade for Christ leader at UCLA. When they met, Barry had

202

no idea how their relationship would take his life in a new direction. Because of his Jewish upbringing, Barry had rejected Jesus as the Messiah. But one day in the student lounge, Hal pulled out a book and showed Barry how Jesus fulfilled Old Testament prophecies.

Barry angrily charged, "Hal, stop using all your Christian books to tell me about Jesus!"

"But, Barry, these aren't my Christian books. I'm reading *your* Jewish Bible—the Old Testament!"

Barry sneered at Hal's words.

"Here," Hal continued. "See for yourself. Take these verses home and look them up in your own Bible."

Reluctantly, Barry took the verses and discovered something he could not deny. The verses Hal had shown Barry in the student lounge were in his Jewish Bible. Hal was right. Old Testament prophecies pointed to Jesus. Not long after their first conversation, Barry confessed Jesus as Messiah, Lord, and Savior.[1]

Barry's story is one of countless like it. What makes this story so meaningful to me is that Barry was Dr. Leventhal, my New Testament professor in seminary. Where did Dr. Leventhal's faith begin? What did Hal share with him that afternoon in the student lounge? The verses of today's prophecy: Isaiah 53.

It Is a Gospel

To this point in our journey, no other Scripture passage that we've studied has foretold Christ's life and ministry more profoundly than Isaiah 53. The gospel writers Matthew, Luke, and John all quote it directly, identifying Jesus as its fulfillment. In Luke's gospel, Jesus quoted Isaiah 53, saying it was fulfilled in him (Luke 22:37). We see so much of Christ's life in the book of Isaiah that the great philosopher and theologian Augustine called it the "fifth Gospel."[2]

Today we will look at this prophecy. We'll walk verse by verse through Isaiah 53 and see Isaiah's description of the Suffering Servant. And as we do, we'll come to Christ and behold the astonishing picture God painted seven hundred years in advance.

The Punishment for Us

Isaiah wrote:

> *He was despised and rejected by men,*
> *a man of sorrows and acquainted with grief;*
> *and as one from whom men hide their faces*
> *he was despised, and we esteemed him not.*
> *(53:3)*

I find it interesting that Isaiah spoke of Christ's suffering as a past event when, in fact, Christ's death and resurrection wouldn't occur for another seven hundred years. To a God not limited by time or space, it only makes sense to see Christ's sufferings and resurrection as something that has already occurred. And it's with this eternal perspective God gave Isaiah the revelation of Christ's life.

Isaiah continued:

> *Surely he has borne our griefs*
> *and carried our sorrows;*
> *yet we esteemed him stricken,*
> *smitten by God, and afflicted.*

Day 17 | He Will Suffer for Me

But he was pierced for our transgressions;
he was crushed for our iniquities.

(vv. 4–5)

Jesus's life was marked by sorrow and grief. Even before his crucifixion, he was betrayed, arrested, mocked, blindfolded, flogged, and
stripped naked.

But Isaiah also made this curious statement about Jesus: "We esteemed
him stricken . . . *by God*." What does he mean? Those who watched
Christ's sufferings thought it was God's judgment descending on a
man who blasphemed God.[3]

But the real reason for Christ's suffering is in the next statement: "He
was pierced for *our* transgressions . . . [and] *our* iniquities." The world
had it wrong. They thought the cross was God's punishment on Christ,
but Jesus was bearing the judgment our sin deserved.

Punishment That Brought Us Peace
While Isaiah's tone to this point had been sorrowful, he continued
with stirring words of hope:

Upon him was the chastisement that brought us peace,
and with his wounds we are healed.

(v. 5)

Peace! His punishment—the beating, scourging, and crucifixion—was not in vain. It was the payment for our peace with God
(Rom. 5:1).

Isaiah 53 also states what none of us would deny—our propensity
to turn away from God:

TRACING HIS PEACE THROUGH PROPHECY

All we like sheep have gone astray;
we have turned—every one—to his own way;
and the LORD has laid on him
the iniquity of us all.

(v. 6)

Isaiah said we each turn to our *own* way. We all sin. My struggles look different from yours. And your struggles look different from those of your boss, pastor, husband, children, sibling, and stranger. Yet we all turn from the Shepherd.

God punishes our sin in an unthinkable way. He laid on *him* the iniquity of us all (v. 6).

Christ's Response

While you and I may resist the Shepherd's leading, Jesus was different. He responded in total surrender. Isaiah said:

He oppressed, and he was afflicted,
yet he opened not his mouth;
like a lamb that is led to the slaughter,
and like a sheep that before its shearers is silent,
so he opened not his mouth.

(v. 7)

Isn't this incredible? Consider Jesus's response to unthinkable afflictions: silence and submission. Think how his response stood in stark contrast to other criminals enduring crucifixion—enraged criminals and murderers yelling profanities and threats, crazed men resisting punishment with all their strength. Jesus was different. Like a gentle lamb, he went quietly to the cross. He said not a word (Matt. 27:14; Mark 15:3–5).

Day 17 | He Will Suffer for Me

Isaiah's prophecy continues with exceptional detail:

> *And they made his grave with the wicked*
> *and with a rich man in his death.*
> *(53:9)*

The wicked *and* the rich. How could this be? The Roman soldiers responsible for Jesus's dead body would have naturally made a grave by the other criminals close to the crucifixion site—with the wicked.[4] But following Jesus's death, the wealthy Joseph of Arimathea asked for Jesus's body and laid it in his own tomb (Matt. 27:57–60). Though the Romans made a grave with wicked men, Jesus was buried with a rich man in his death.

Isaiah continued by speaking of Jesus's innocence, which New Testament authors affirm (2 Cor. 5:21; Heb. 4:15; 1 John 3:5):

> *Although he had done no violence,*
> *and there was no deceit in his mouth.*
>
> *Yet it was the will of the Lord to crush him.*
> *(vv. 9–10)*

No violence. No deceit. Sinless. This is key. If Jesus were not sinless, then his death and resurrection would have done nothing to remove our sins. He would have been just another man dying on a cross.

What an intriguing statement: "Yet it was the will of the Lord to crush him" (v. 10). Other translations say it *pleased* the Lord to crush him (NKJV, NASB95).

Jesus's crucifixion was God's plan. It wasn't a catastrophic accident ending his life. He wasn't a moral leader whose agenda turned sour. This was the sovereign hand of God—at the perfect time and in the perfect way—offering his Son as a sacrifice to save the world from sin.

His Resurrection, Our Redemption

We often think Isaiah 53 only describes the sufferings of Jesus. But as we finish, I want to show one more section that brings a perfect end to this part of our study.

> *When his soul makes an offering for guilt,*
> *he shall see his offspring; he shall prolong his days;*
> *the will of the LORD shall prosper in his hand.*
> *Out of the anguish of his soul he shall see and be satisfied.*
> *(vv. 10–11)*

Do you hear the delight in Isaiah's voice? Though God made Jesus an offering, Jesus will see his offspring—those who believe in him—and be satisfied because his work on the cross was complete.[5]

Then, notice how the perspective shifts from Isaiah speaking to God speaking. The text speaks from God's perspective, calling Jesus "my servant":

> *By his knowledge shall the righteous one, my servant,*
> *make many to be accounted righteous,*
> *and he shall bear their iniquities.*

(v. 11)

Accounted righteous. Remember God's promise to Abraham in Genesis 15 (day 4)? God promised Abraham that all the nations of the earth would be blessed through him. Abraham believed, and God accounted him righteous—a picture of salvation through faith. One thousand years later, God revealed that his servant, the Seed, would make many righteous—not through works, but because Christ bore their iniquities, taking the punishment for their sin!

Truth and Trust

How could it be God's desire for Jesus to suffer? How could this please him? One word.

Love.

"For God so loved the world, that he gave his only Son, that whoever believes in him should not perish but have eternal life" (John 3:16). It pleased the Lord to crush him because God knew the outcome of Jesus's suffering—our relationship with him.

In a world that trains us to strive, stress, and achieve, we need to remember God's amazing love. Our acceptance is not based on performance, position, or perfection. We are loved. *You* are loved, because you are his child. Jesus paid the penalty for your imperfections.

> Our acceptance is not based on performance, position, or perfection. We are loved. You are loved, because you are his child.

As we come to him and know his love, we experience his peace and rest for our souls (Matt. 11:28–30). Not fragmented thoughts, concerns, and worries, but peace—knowing God loves us, is in control, and we are in right standing with him.

It was God's love that placed Jesus on the cross. God's love also moved the prophet Isaiah to write Isaiah 53. Through it we can have confidence in the Old Testament—confidence regarding its certainty and divine authorship.

This was the confidence that Dr. Leventhal needed to receive Jesus as his Savior.

It could be the same confidence you, your spouse, your children, your sibling, or someone you know needs to trust in Jesus.

It's the confidence that God loves us and sent a Redeemer.

His Son.
The Seed.
His name is Jesus.
He invites all to come to him.

Of all the details Isaiah foretold in Isaiah 53, which one is the most meaningful to you?

How does this prophecy give you confidence in the Scriptures?

Sometimes we can fall into patterns of guilt and shame. How does seeing the extent to which Jesus suffered so we might be forgiven help you in the areas where you may be prone to carry guilt?

JESSE TREE
What is something you want to remember about Isaiah 53?

TRACING
HIS
Plan
THROUGH
HISTORY

Day 18

BETHLEHEM:
GOD IS IN THE DETAILS

Read Micah 5:2; Acts 17:26–28.

$\mathcal{M}$ost girls dream of a glittery happily-ever-after life. I was no exception. Ryan and I had our first conversation one afternoon following choir practice, and by evening I was rehearsing my first name with his last.

However, I never expected the challenge that we'd face during our first two years as bride and groom. It was more than finances or laundry folding—it was an unexpected and trying test of faith.

Only weeks before Ryan and I were married, he enrolled in a religion class as part of his training for ministry. But Ryan's university professor wasn't like the favorite Sunday school teacher you may remember from church—flannelgraph and easel in tow. She had been a Christian—a nun in fact—and had left the faith. From the first class, her questions and attacks against Christianity chipped away at Ryan's once-thriving faith. Rather than spur Ryan to Jesus, she planted seeds of doubt and disbelief.

Though my excitement about our upcoming wedding grew stronger, so did my gnawing concern for Ryan. Six weeks into the semester, we were married. His questions about Christianity intensified, and I knew he was struggling. He began reaching out to pastors and Christian leaders, longing for answers. Unfortunately, responses like "just have faith" and "repent" were not what he needed.

By the end of the semester—only a few months into our marriage—Ryan confessed to me that he could not, in good conscience, continue the path of ministry. More than that, he could no longer call himself a follower of Jesus.

My heart broke. This was *not* the way it was supposed to be. I wondered if I had made a mistake and whom I could confide in. In one semester I had watched my shiny dream dim under the dark cloud of Ryan's struggle—a struggle for truth.

Life has a way of bringing the unexpected, doesn't it? I don't know the situations surrounding your story, but I'm learning that when the unexpected comes, we can find comfort in knowing nothing is a surprise to God and he has a plan.

Day 18 | Bethlehem: God Is in the Details

I believe this is no better demonstrated than in the study of prophecy. It's a powerful reminder that though we can't see the big picture, God does. And because our all-knowing God is also all loving and all powerful, we can rest, knowing he orchestrates events to further his divine purpose.

Micah's Prophecy

Yesterday we ended with Isaiah's prophecy of Christ's sufferings in Isaiah 53. Today we'll look at a prophecy from Micah that unveils a fascinating detail about the place of Christ's birth. Like other prophecies we've studied, Micah's is written in poetry, where inanimate objects are often personified: the sun smiles, the trees clap their hands, the hills rejoice. Fun, right?

Micah's prophecy is no different, as he personifies a small yet significant town in Israel—Bethlehem. But the town doesn't speak, smile, or clap. Instead, Micah addresses the town as if it were a *person* to prepare it for what would come:

> *But you, O Bethlehem Ephrathah,*
> *who are too little to be among the clans of Judah,*
> *from you shall come forth for me*
> *one who is to be ruler in Israel,*
> *whose coming forth is from of old,*
> *from ancient days.*
> (5:2)

Here, Micah speaks to the town of Bethlehem, saying that from it shall come the "ruler in Israel." Notice how the verse ends: "Whose coming forth is from of old, from ancient days." Other translations say "from everlasting" (NKJV) or "days of eternity" (NASB95).

Days of eternity. This brief phrase unlocks the significance of Micah's prophecy. The One born in Bethlehem would be no ordinary ruler. He would be from eternity past. Not only that, God said the ruler would be "for me." That is, he would come to serve God's purposes.

I marvel at how Micah, while prophesying Christ's physical birthplace, captured both the heart of Christ's purpose (for God) and the eternality of his existence.

A Peek into the New Testament

We understand the significance of Micah's prophecy now, but what about the people during the time Jesus was born? Did they know? Come with me to the New Testament, where shortly after the birth of Jesus, King Herod asked the Jewish leaders about the Christ child's location.

> *[King Herod] inquired of them where the Christ was to be born. They told him, "In Bethlehem of Judea, for so it is written by the prophet:*
> *'And you, O Bethlehem . . .*
> *from you shall come a ruler*
>   *who will shepherd my people Israel.'"*
> *(Matt. 2:4–6)*

Don't you love how Scripture comes together? Seven hundred years after Micah spoke of Bethlehem, the Jewish leaders remembered this prophecy and used it to answer the question of Jesus's birthplace.

He Performs His Word

You may think Micah's prophecy isn't that unusual. After all, King David was from Bethlehem. It would only make sense that Jesus would be born in the same town as David. But this is where it gets interesting. At the time of Mary's pregnancy, Joseph and Mary were not residents of Bethlehem. Not even close. They lived in Nazareth—ninety miles away.

Day 18 | Bethlehem: God Is in the Details

But Micah said the Christ child would be born in Bethlehem. To fulfill this prophecy, God would need to compel the couple to make a multiday trek from Nazareth to Bethlehem at the precise time of Jesus's birth.

What would cause Joseph and Mary to make this journey, especially with Mary so close to delivering? The Christmas story tells us what was happening in that part of the world at the time: "In those days a decree went out from Caesar Augustus that all the world should be registered.... And all went to be registered, each to his own town. And Joseph also went up ... to the city of David, which is called Bethlehem" (Luke 2:1, 3–4).

These verses may be familiar, but what they tell us is important. Caesar's taxation required everyone to travel to their own town—their ancestral town. Because Joseph was of the lineage of David, he and Mary had to travel from Nazareth to Bethlehem to fulfill Caesar's decree.

If Joseph and Mary had not gone to Bethlehem, Mary would have given birth to Jesus in Nazareth, not Bethlehem. But God, at the perfect time, moved Caesar Augustus to issue widespread taxation. What appeared to be a political mandate from Caesar was a sovereign act of God, transferring the woman carrying his Seed to the prophesied location of the Messiah's birth!

Isn't this incredible? God relocated Mary and Joseph ninety uncomfortable miles to fulfill a promise he had spoken seven hundred years earlier. God would not let his promise go unfulfilled.

Or to view it from another faith-building perspective: the all-knowing, all-seeing God knew Joseph and Mary would be in Bethlehem during the taxation and gave that revelation to Micah seven hundred years in advance. Let's just let that sink in a moment.

God has a perspective we do not have, and he does what he says he will do. His promises have power. He knows all and sees all. We don't have to wonder and worry if God will act. He watches over his word to perform it (Jer. 1:12).

Is there a situation in your life that has you troubled? Is there a promise you're believing as you wait? Are you trusting for his provision? If you feel uncertain about how to walk in those promises or could use fresh inspiration, you will find a list of promises to pray in appendix D. It is a wonderful way to come to God confidently as his child.

Holding All Things Together

My happily-ever-after life wasn't unfolding as I had expected. But hope sparked one weekend when Ryan took a road trip with high school friends. During the drive, Ryan sat with Jason, who just happened to be studying to be a pastor. More than that, Jason had a passion for apologetics—a study that answers the tough questions asked of Christianity. The very questions plaguing Ryan's mind.

As they talked, Ryan voiced his questions, and Jason had answers—solid, logical, and biblical. Additionally, Jason suggested a list of Christian books to satisfy Ryan's God-given curiosity and passion for truth.

Now over twenty years later, Ryan continues to walk with Jesus, has served over ten years in full-time ministry, and even earned a degree in apologetics to help others with similar struggles. (As a fun side note, Ryan's friend—Jason Jimenez—is now an author, apologist, and the founder of Stand Strong Ministries.)

While our story had a happy ending, it was a rocky road. Sometimes we think life should be pretty, perfect, and packaged well. But trials happen and hard times come. And the truth is, even when we feel like tensing up in fear, Christ invites us again and again to a warm relationship of loving trust.

Why? Because he holds all things together.

And he's holding you as well.

Truth and Trust

The events surrounding Micah 5:2 demonstrate a timeless truth: God orchestrates events to fulfill his divine purpose. What we may interpret as a natural event or unexpected setback could be a supernatural God at work.

Never think that the specifics of where and when you live are without purpose. Your street, school, church, job, and relationships are all part of God's plan. Just as God sovereignly arranged the details for Mary and Joseph, he sovereignly designs the details of ours. Paul said this perfectly:

> *[God] made from one man every nation of mankind to live on all the face of the earth, having determined allotted periods and the boundaries of their dwelling place, that they should seek God, and perhaps feel their way toward him and find him. Yet he is actually not far from each one of us. (Acts 17:26–27)*

God is the one who determines when and where we live, placing us in the exact location of his choosing. And it's not without purpose. We may think we live somewhere because of a job opportunity, family relationship, school situation, less traffic, or good weather. Paul revealed the real reason: that we would seek after God and find him.

Whether you are in transition, in trial, settled, or somewhere in between, your heavenly Father is behind the scenes, aligning your life's details because he has given you a unique assignment.

Be assured of this: There is purpose to your path. Even the delays, even the seasons of waiting, even in that middle place, even in the valleys, God is arranging and working in ways we cannot see. As we respond to the invitation to reach out to God and find him, he promises to draw near to us (James 4:8). As a result, we'll move from simply believing God to *experiencing* the reality of his all-encompassing involvement in our lives.

There is purpose to your path.

Today, take a deep breath and let the events surrounding Micah 5:2 and Christ's birth bring confidence to your heart. God's blueprint is in place. He promises grace for every situation. We can trust his promises and his timing. What we may consider natural events and setbacks might just be God's supernatural way of advancing his plan ... so we can know him more.

Want to know the nearness of God?

> Embrace your place.
> Trust his timing.
> Cling to his strength.
> Seek after him.

He is not far from you.

Would you describe yourself as settled, transitioning, or somewhere in between? What lessons about God are you learning along the way?

Paul said in Acts that God places us where we are so we can seek him and find him. How does this change how you think about the town where you live? Your school? Workplace? Neighborhood?

When you think about the fulfillment of Micah's prophecy, how does it help you look at your current circumstance or struggle and God's divine plan in a new way?

JESSE TREE
What is something you want to remember about Micah's prophecy?

Day 19

NEW COVENANT:
CHANGE IS COMING

Read Jeremiah 31:31–34; Hebrews 10:4, 11–18.

’ll never forget the first time I took a youth group on an overnight camping trip. I was young, hip (not really), and a rookie to the world of student ministry. I'll be honest—the thought of leading *anything* overnight with teenagers sounded terrifying.

At the end of the first day, the girls went to the cabin for the night.

About an hour or two later, the hum of giggles and conversation died down, and everyone appeared to be asleep.

Not me. I was restless and wired, trying to find solace in the squeaky cabin bunk. I checked the clock—1:00 a.m. Just as I was falling asleep, the front screen door swung open. I popped up and saw a shadowy figure slip down the stairs of the front porch and vanish.

My immediate reaction was to tell the person in charge. Then I remembered, *Oh no. I am the person in charge.*

I ventured down the porch stairs into the moonlit woods in search of the runaway girl. No luck. I sat on the porch and waited. Forty-five minutes later, Courtney slowly approached the cabin. Now I *really* didn't know what to do.

As she trudged up the stairs, our eyes met. "Courtney, what did you do?" I asked.

"I snuck out. It was wrong. I'm sorry."

My mind searched for what to say next. "Courtney, what did you do *wrong?*"

To my surprise, she went into *more* detail.

"What else did you do?" I asked.

Courtney responded with more details.

"What else did you do?" I asked again.

The question kept working, so I kept asking. By the end of our conversation, Courtney felt the weight of her poor decision, and I realized I had a lot to learn about student ministry.

As I think back to that night, I realize my goal was not to bring restoration to Courtney. My questions only created condemnation and shame. Sure, Courtney needed correction. But rather than soften her heart through love and forgiveness, I focused on her failure and faults, which created distance.

Have you ever thought we may view God the same way? As if he prefers wrath over restoration? As if he's in heaven asking, "What else did you do wrong?"

But here's what we must remember: God is a God of grace and forgiveness. He doesn't desire distance but relationship and reconciliation (2 Cor. 5:19).

We'll see this in full view as we move into one of the most thrilling days of our study—the new covenant. For a nation and people in rebellion's pit, God promised to do something new. Together, we'll unearth two Old Testament prophecies about this new way God would interact with the world.

And as we unpack the Scriptures, we'll also watch how Jesus brilliantly fulfilled these prophecies. It's a stunning picture of our salvation and the confidence we can have through a grace-filled relationship with Jesus.

The Prophecy: A New Heart
We begin with what God spoke through the prophet Jeremiah:

> *Behold, the days are coming, declares the* LORD, *when I will*
> *make a new covenant with the house of Israel and the house*

of Judah. . . . I will put my law within them, and I will write it on their hearts. (Jer. 31:31, 33)

Pause and think of the significance of this statement. For hundreds of years, God's people had been under the old covenant, or Mosaic law. As much as they intended to keep the law, they chased the laser light of the world's idols and allurements. As a result, God brought his hand of discipline.

But Jeremiah prophesied a message of hope. God would make a *new* covenant.

Under the old covenant, the law had been a code of morals, external to man. Paul described it as a ministry of death and condemnation (2 Cor. 3:7–9). But in the new covenant, God would shape people's character from within. The laws would not be written on stone tablets but traced by God on the human heart.

Along with the law being on our hearts, the prophet Ezekiel spoke of another promise regarding the new covenant: "I will give you a new hcart. . . . I will put my Spirit within you, and cause you to walk in my statutes and be careful to obey my rules" (Ezek. 36:26–27).

A new *heart.* The Spirit *within* you. What did this all mean? With the new covenant, God would instill power in every believer—the person of the Holy Spirit—enabling and empowering believers to follow God's heart and plan.

No Favorites or VIPs

When our kids were little, they rarely waited for permission to go anywhere, especially to see their dad at work. We'd arrive at the church and Charity and Isaiah would swing open the doors and race full throttle to their dad's office. They'd jump on his lap, tell him about their day, and snuggle in his arms.

No call or appointment needed. Because of their relationship, they enjoyed full intimacy and access to their daddy's arms. Anytime.

The closeness my children experience with their dad is unlike what Israel experienced with God. Under the old covenant, a divide existed between everyday people and the priests, and between people and God. Only the priest had access to the holy place and God's presence.

But in the new covenant, this chasm would be bridged. The playing field of spirituality would be leveled. No favorites or VIPs. No distance.

Regarding the new covenant, Jeremiah prophesied, "For they shall all know me, from the least of them to the greatest, declares the Lord. For I will forgive their iniquity, and I will remember their sin no more" (Jer. 31:34).

They shall *all* know God. How? Forgiveness. What once required sacrifices, rituals, and the mediator of a priest, God would accomplish through Jesus in the new covenant. Like a child running into their father's arms, forgiveness allows all to draw near to God. The priest, the poor, the college student, the empty nester, the mom, the dad, and the Amazon driver. All can draw near. Hallelujah!

The New Testament Connection

When teaching the big picture of the Bible, I encourage people to think of Scripture like a two-act play: the Old Testament and New Testament. As with any play or movie, understanding the foundation of the Old Testament (act 1) makes familiar scenes of the New Testament (act 2) breathe with fresh vibrancy.

Now that we've seen Old Testament promises of the new covenant, we'll pull up to the table at Jesus's final meal with his disciples—the Last Supper. Here, we'll grasp the profound significance in Jesus's familiar words before his crucifixion. You'll love this.

Toward the end of the meal, Jesus took the cup and told his disciples, "This cup that is poured out for you is the *new covenant* in my blood" (Luke 22:20). Isn't this incredible? This wasn't any cup—it was the cup of the new covenant.

Jesus said it similarly in Matthew: "For this is my blood of *the covenant*, which is poured out for many for the forgiveness of sins" (26:28).

In this moment Jesus announced he was the one through whom the new covenant would come. Jesus's blood would inaugurate the prophecy Jeremiah and Ezekiel had spoken six hundred years earlier.[1]

It only gets better. Jesus's sacrifice opened a new way for us to approach God. In the Old Testament, when the high priest went before God's presence, he passed through a massive veil—symbolizing the barrier between man and God.

I always pictured this veil as a thin sheet or curtain, but the veil was unbelievably huge. It soared sixty feet high, stretched thirty feet wide, and may have been as thick as a person's hand (about four inches thick).[2]

At the precise moment of Christ's death on the cross, something incredible happened to this veil: "The curtain of the temple was torn in two, from top to bottom. And the earth shook, and the rocks were split" (Matt. 27:51). Picture the moment. The massive curtain towering five stories high ripped from top to bottom.

Some people say the earthquake caused the splitting, but the order is noteworthy: the curtain was torn, the earth shook, and the rocks split. What if God tearing the curtain caused the earth to shake? What if his announcement for all to come into his presence rocked the world?

And did you notice the veil was torn from top to bottom? This was not a work of man but of the hand of God.[3]

> **What if his announcement for all to come into his presence rocked the world?**

Using the stunning image of the torn veil, the author of Hebrews revealed how this image of the torn veil impacts you and me—how *we* can now enter God's presence: "Since we have confidence to enter the holy places by the blood of Jesus, by the new and living way that he opened for us through the curtain, that is, through his flesh. . . . let us draw near" (10:19–20, 22).

The curtain. The flesh. Drawing near. They all come together. It's a past event that points to a present reality. Jesus's death on the cross removed the barrier between God and man. Tearing the curtain was God's holy and grand invitation for us to know and enjoy his presence. In the words of Jeremiah, for all to know him. What a thought.

Confidence to enter. The more I study the new covenant, the more I realize our confidence is not based on our work but on Christ's. Think with me. The covenant, the sacrifice, the blood, the cup, the curtain—these are all steps God took toward us, granting us access to his presence.

Truth and Trust

Let me ask you a question: How would you say you come before God? We might admit that "boldly" or "with confidence" is not always our approach. I know I would. Sometimes we come half-heartedly or timidly. We might come distracted or lacking faith. We might come to God discouraged because the mountain before us seems impassable. We avoid asking God for help because we doubt he'll do anything. Or sometimes, like Courtney, the decisions of our past weigh on us, and we come with shame or guilt.

But know this, my friend: God has a better way. Whatever you've done—the decisions you made last week, last year, or ten years ago, or even the decisions you feel robbed years from your life—these are all forgiven through Jesus. Completely. There is no condemnation (Rom. 8:1).

As people of the new covenant—forgiven and filled with God's Spirit—the acceptance and love we receive from God is not based on our good deeds or living a perfect life. We are accepted because of Christ's work.

Like a child running into their father's arms, we have bold and beautiful access to God. Shame melts. Guilt disappears. Regrets die. Worship is rich. We enter with passion, reverence, and awe because Christ made a way.

> ### Shame melts. Guilt disappears.
> ### Regrets die. Worship is rich.

Jesus isn't sitting on the cabin porch, waiting for you to return so he can rehearse your wrongdoings. He's not going to heap on guilt or condemnation.

If my husband delights in our children running into his arms, how much more does our heavenly Father delight as we come to him?

What if today you went before him with confidence? Not arrogantly. Not irreverently. But boldly because the barrier is gone.

Sin is forgiven.
He's given his Spirit.
We have confidence to come boldly.
All can know him.

Questions

If you were to describe how you come before God, what would you say? Confidently? Timidly? Shamefully?

What is your biggest hindrance to coming to God with more confidence?

How does the image of the veil tearing from top to bottom speak to you personally?

What do you sense God saying to you through today's teaching?

JESSE TREE

What is something you want to remember about the new covenant?

Day 20

EXILE:
THE FOURTH MAN IN THE FIRE

Read Daniel 3.

After moving so many times as a family, Ryan and I were thrilled when our daughter found a group of friends that made her eyes sparkle. We couldn't have been happier. The families were close, and we loved seeing her in community when the previous years had been so chaotic and isolating.

However, after time we noticed that these friends began drifting in a direction that did not honor God. For Ryan and me, the question wasn't as much about whether their actions were biblical—it was what our response would be. We had long conversations, playing out the risk of staying versus the loss of leaving: the relationships, the hurt feelings, the tough conversations, and removing Charity from the friends she loved.

It was a test—a test of whether we would hold to our convictions or conform to the culture.

If you've been a Christian for any amount of time, you know life can feel like a series of tests. Tests like, Will we trust God to answer the prayer or believe him to provide a need? Will we believe him for grace and peace through a challenging season?

But sometimes we experience a different kind of test. A test where we must choose whether to hold to our convictions or slip down the slope of compromise.

If you're a parent, you may feel pressured to let your kids participate in activities that violate your conscience. In a work environment colleagues might try to coerce you into compromising actions. Or if you're single, you might feel the pressure to relax your standards in relationships.

Or perhaps it's a struggle no one sees. You may feel pulled by the allurement of social media or the temptation to bow to the culture in what's central to your thoughts and how you spend your time.

If you've felt these tensions, you know it's a challenging place. And usually it's not a question of what would be pleasing to God or what is the right thing to do. That answer is obvious. More often, the question is, What will following my convictions cost me? What's at stake? Will I lose my job? Friends? Fun? Will people think I'm too rigid?

In weightier situations you may ask, How will my decision impact my family? Can I handle the stress of doing the right thing when it would be easier to stay silent and conform to the culture or wishes of those around me?

Sometimes it's a test where once we decide to do the right thing, there's no turning back. We may be at the mercy of those whose agenda we threatened. If we go against their desires, we're unsure of what will happen next.

The outcome is unknown.

Have you or someone you love been there? Perhaps you're there now.

This was the situation for Shadrach, Meshach, and Abednego. Exiled from their home country, these young men lived in a culture blatantly opposed to God. There, they would face the ultimate test.

Today we'll watch how their faith moved them to challenges, uncertainty, and ultimately to the greatest gift of all—a revelation of their Savior.

The Challenge

At this point in our journey through the Old Testament, the Assyrians have conquered the Northern Kingdom of Israel, and the Southern Kingdom's destruction by Babylon is looming. Today, our camera lens focuses on a fascinating scene several years before the fall of the Southern Kingdom of Judah.

In 605 BC King Nebuchadnezzar of Babylon selected young men from

Judah to serve in his royal court. These youths were to be "without blemish, of good appearance and skillful in all wisdom, endowed with knowledge, understanding learning, and competent to stand in the king's palace" (Dan. 1:4). Studs, basically. Among these men were Daniel, Shadrach, Meshach, and Abednego.

In Daniel 3 King Nebuchadnezzar made an image of gold. This was no small statue or portable pocket charm. It towered ninety feet tall—the height of an eight-story building.[1] Then he invited—or commanded— all his officials and administrators to attend a dedication ceremony for the statue.

On the day of the statue's dedication, the king's herald belted out these instructions: "When you hear the sound of . . . every kind of music, you are to fall down and worship the golden image. . . . And whoever does not fall down and worship shall immediately be cast into a burning fiery furnace" (Dan. 3:5–6).

Intense, isn't it? Imagine the scene. Thousands of people falling to the ground to worship the statue.

No doubt, this would have been a significant test for Shadrach, Meshach, and Abednego. As Jews, they followed the Ten Commandments—the first two of which forbade idolatry. Would these exiled men compromise and live, or would they remain faithful and possibly die?

The Fear Factor

It's interesting that we know nothing of Shadrach, Meshach, and Abednego's thoughts or feelings. I often wonder how hard the decision was for them. Had they heard of the decree in advance and anticipated this day would come? Had they stayed up late discussing their options? If it were me, I would have lost sleep as I considered the punishment, flinching at the very thought of fiery death.

As I envision the people bowing before the statue, my guess is that they followed the king's decree more out of fear than heartfelt allegiance to a nation or king. And rightly so—rebellion meant being burned alive.

At the same time, I wonder how often we bow to the culture because of fear. Fear of man. Fear of the unknown. Fear of loss. Fearing how people will respond or how inconvenient our decision will make our life.

We're not facing fiery furnaces, but we may lose our job, relationships, or popularity. We fear mockery, isolation, or simply the unknown.

This was the case in our situation with Charity. We feared the uncomfortable conversations and what the other parents would say. We were concerned we'd be misunderstood. We feared Charity's reaction and if she could find another group of friends.

Weeks and months passed with no clear direction, until one afternoon I'll never forget. The house was empty, and I had been in the home office struggling to get work done. Overwhelmed, I closed my computer, slid out of my chair onto my knees, and asked God for wisdom.

Within only a minute or two of praying, the answer came. I saw a mental picture of Charity wearing the armor of God. My spiritual senses fixed on the breastplate of righteousness. With that simple picture, the answer was clear. If we wanted Charity to walk in God's protection and peace, we should choose righteousness and let that be her guard. Any other attempt at compromise—or simply staying silent and hoping for the best—was not an option.

We didn't need to fear the future. We didn't need to worry about what other parents would say or how they would react. We didn't need to fear the transition Charity would have to make. We would choose to obey, and God would choose the outcome.

Even If He Does Not Deliver Us

I would have loved to have been in Babylon the day Shadrach, Meshach, and Abednego decided to stand—three striking young men standing tall among the sea of bowing people. I wonder if their knees trembled with fear and their hearts pounded in their chests. Did their palms drip with sweat and their faces flush over the attention they couldn't avoid? Perhaps their eyes pooled with tears as they envisioned their pending punishment. Still, Shadrach, Meshach, and Abednego stood tall.

It wasn't long before word of their actions reached King Nebuchadnezzar. Enraged, the king brought them into his presence. He asked what god would save them from the fire. I love their surrendered response: "If we are thrown into the blazing furnace, the God we serve is able to deliver us from it, and he will deliver us. . . . But even if he does not . . . we will not serve your gods or worship the image of gold you have set up" (Dan. 3:17–18 NIV).

Don't you love this? "But *even if* he does not." With unwavering convictions and belief in the impossible, the three men told the king they would worship God alone.

We can let this be a lesson for us. These three men's response teaches that we should build our worship on the altar of expectation but on the sovereignty of God's perfect plan. It's easy to trust God for a particular outcome and agonize over his answer, but Shadrach, Meshach, and Abednego didn't cave under uncertainty. They were determined worshipers, mature enough to know God might not answer as they desired. And yet they worshiped God alone, trusting his plan would bring him the most glory.

Truth and Trust

As promised, King Nebuchadnezzar bound the three men and cast them into the blazing flames, but what happened next was astounding. The king jumped up and asked his officials, "Did we not cast three men bound into the fire? . . . I see four men unbound, walking in the midst of the fire, and they are not hurt; and the appearance of the fourth is like a son of the gods" (Dan. 3:24–25).

These young men were not alone! King Nebuchadnezzar saw not three but *four* men walking in the flames—unbound and free.

I love today's study. We're not looking at a prophecy, promise, or foreshadowing of Jesus. We're seeing what many theologians believe is an appearance of Christ *before* he took on humanity. It was Jesus with them in the fire.[2]

Through the miracle of the fiery furnace, God gave Shadrach, Meshach, and Abednego a glimpse of what had been there the whole time—Christ's presence in their lives. He was there. He had been there the entire time.

He was there when they were exiled from their home to a foreign land. He was there when they stood and others bowed. He was there when they were thrown into the flames. Christ was there, empowering them to walk in a fire they could only survive by his supernatural touch.

He is with us as well. He's there when you have a challenging conversation with your boss or talk to your boyfriend about honoring God in your relationship. He's there when you share your concerns for your children's innocence with the school's administration. He's there when you feel alone because your friends walk the path of compromise. He's there when you guide your teenagers through decisions that honor God. He's there when you make the right decision, even when no one else sees.

Is there an area where God is calling you to follow your convictions and not the crowd? A place where the world is bending its knee to the idols of our day? What would it look like for you to not bow to the culture but honor God through your decisions?

It takes courage to stand when the rest of the world is bending the knee. Obedience often requires we go against the culture, and it doesn't promise the easiest path. At the same time, it opens the door for God to reveal himself in ways we may have never experienced otherwise.

God may not spare us from the fire, but he promises his presence as we walk through it (Isa. 43:2). And the best part? God's revelation is greatest in the fire—to us and those watching our lives.

May our hearts always worship, even in the fire!

Questions

Recall a time when you have faced a decision to compromise or hold to your convictions. What did you learn through it?

As you read this chapter, did a current situation come to mind?

Do you feel as if part of the struggle to hold strong to Scripture comes from fear? Fear of people? Fear of the unknown? Or fear of . . . ?

Think of a trusted Christian friend with whom you could share your struggle. Ask him or her to pray for you to have the strength to make the right choice.

If a friend of yours were facing your current situation or temptation, what advice would you give?

JESSE TREE

What is something you want to remember about the fiery furnace?

Day 21

RETURN FROM EXILE: STRENGTH FOR GOD'S WORK

Read Ezra 1:1–3; 4:1–5; Nehemiah 6:15–16.

After another long day of chasing toddlers around the house and working two part-time jobs from home, I was *exhausted*. It was that season of life when collapsing in bed often feels like the highlight of the day.

I carried Charity to bed and cuddled with her to read stories and say prayers. In the quietness of that moment, I asked, "Charity, can you think of one thing you want to thank God for?"

She thought for a moment, looked up with her big brown eyes, and said, "Mom, I want to thank God for 'just a minute.'"

"Just a minute? What do you mean you're thankful for 'just a minute'?"

She answered, "When I need your help and call out for you and you say, 'just a minute,' then I know you've heard me. You'll be there soon to help. So I'm thankful for 'just a minute.'"

As I stroked her silky brown hair, I smiled at the beauty of her heart and knew her words were the Spirit's whisper to me that evening. But God wasn't "just a minute" away or busy somewhere else. He was right there with me. He had been there all along—in my exhaustion, fatigue, and frustration.

The comforting message of God's nearness is what the Israelites would need for the next part of their journey. Though there would be excitement, there would also be frustration, discouragement, and opposition. Still, God remained near.

Yesterday we watched the faith of Shadrach, Meshach, and Abednego at the beginning of the Babylonian exile. Today we view the broader picture of history and see that the exile that began with these young men ultimately extended to the rest of the Southern Kingdom of Judah.

In 586 BC God used Babylon as his tool of discipline to exile the Jewish people to a foreign land.

We read the words quickly, but imagine the devastation. Watching your home and nation leveled by invaders, seeing your place of worship become a pile of rubble, and being forced away from the place you love. But while God allowed discipline and destruction, he also ordained a new destiny for his people—returning to the land to rebuild the temple and city walls.

Today we make the last stop on our journey through the Old Testament. We'll learn rich and relevant lessons as we watch the Israelite people know his nearness and put their hands to the work of their God.

The Decree

At this point in our study of the Old Testament, Judah has been exiled, and their Babylonian conquerors have been defeated by Persia. King Cyrus of Persia sits on the throne of the most powerful nation in the world.

During the first year of Cyrus's reign, something incredible happened: "In order to fulfill the word of the LORD spoken by Jeremiah, the LORD moved the heart of Cyrus king of Persia to make a proclamation" (Ezra 1:1 NIV). Notice *who* was moving Cyrus's heart. This was the Lord's doing.

Cyrus decreed, "Any of his people among you may go up to Jerusalem in Judah and rebuild the temple of the LORD" (v. 3 NIV).

Pause and think of the significance of this decree. After years of exile, God stirred a *pagan* king to release God's people to build a place of worship in Jerusalem! What's more, Cyrus released God's people as a fulfillment of Jeremiah's prophecy (v. 1). Years earlier, Jeremiah prophesied Judah's destruction, the release of the people from captivity, and even how long the exile would last (Jer. 29:10). Incredible.

There's more. Jeremiah wasn't the only one who spoke of the release from exile. The prophet Isaiah said King Cyrus would proclaim that

Day 21 | Return from Exile: Strength for God's Work

Jerusalem "shall be built" and the temple foundation "shall be laid" (Isa. 44:28). Are you seeing this? Jeremiah prophesied the length of the exile, and Isaiah foretold *by name* who would initiate the release.

This excites me. I don't know about you, but it's easy to get so entangled in day-to-day living that we forget God knows all things and is sovereign over all things. God is the only one who could predict the length of captivity. He's the only one who could stir a pagan king's heart. And God is the only one who could show Isaiah that a king named Cyrus would initiate the end of captivity 150 years before it happened.[1]

And for us, God is the only one who knows our story and has a perspective we don't have. He's the only one who can stir the hearts of those we are praying for. He's the only one who wrote our days in his book before any of them came to be (Ps. 139:16).

Nothing about our lives is outside his knowledge or his care. The concerns keeping you awake at night, the past circumstances that perplex you, or the future events that concern you—God has them in his hands, and he is with you.

Sword in One Hand and Tool in the Other

Now that Judah had the decree, it would be fun to say the people skipped off to Jerusalem, renovated the temple HGTV-style, and everyone lived happily ever after. But that's not what happened. During the temple's reconstruction, enemies "discouraged the people . . . and made them afraid to build" (Ezra 4:4). These enemies were so successful that the people stopped building altogether. This wasn't a safety sweep or three-day weekend. Because of the enemy's assaults, progress stopped for over fifteen years.[2]

Similarly, during the reconstruction of Jerusalem's wall some years later, another group of enemies attacked God's people with ridicule, mockery, slander, and threats of taking their leader Nehemiah's life. For those working the wall, it required them to build with one hand and hold a weapon in the other (Neh. 4:17).

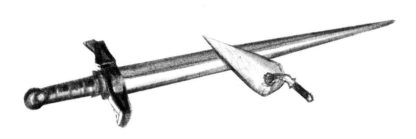

Does this surprise you like it does me? Hadn't God released his people and decreed the rebuild? Hadn't he foretold their return and stirred a foreign king to decree his people's release? Rebuilding Jerusalem was God's plan. The people were walking in obedience. It shouldn't have been that hard, right?

It's interesting that the enemies did not destroy or annihilate the Jewish people. Their tactics were different. They used conniving threats, jeering remarks, and slanderous words to sour the people's joy and confidence in doing God's work. The Enemy wouldn't destroy them entirely, but he would harass them incessantly.

Sadly, it worked. For the Jewish people, fear was their constant companion, and discouragement was the weight they bore.

Do you ever feel a similar discouragement? You set out with a directive from God, yet experience fear, frustration, and false accusation.

Day 21 | Return from Exile: Strength for God's Work

You are doing work for God's glory—raising your kids, being a witness at work or school, serving at church, or leading a small group—and things take longer than you expect or more energy than you anticipated. You're discouraged and wonder why things aren't easier.

These tactics are how the Enemy comes against us. Through whispers masked as our own thoughts, the Enemy drives us to a place of such discouragement that giving up or stopping seems like the only option. He makes us think the work won't be worth it, we don't have what it takes—or even worse, God is not in it. If the Enemy can't discourage us, he'll distract us. Or he'll try for both.

This was the case for the people of Israel. They had God's green light to return and rebuild Jerusalem, but the opposition was overwhelming. Ease and steady progress may have been Israel's expectation, but resistance was their reality.

> If the Enemy can't discourage us, he'll distract us. Or he'll try for both.

Should we think it will be any different for us?

Thankfully, there are seasons when the wind is behind our sails. But in many cases, progressing in God's plan requires us to carry a sword to fight the Enemy in one hand and a tool for God's work in the other.

Now Is the Time

The good news is that the people completed the temple under Zerubbabel's leadership, and later under Nehemiah they finished the wall around Jerusalem.[3]

As an interesting side note, many families remained in Persia despite Cyrus's decree, and they stayed there for generations to come. Two you may know by name—Mordecai and his cousin Esther, who later married a Persian king and became queen. The book of Esther details her reign and how God used her to save the Jewish people from annihilation. How's that for a fun fact?

While we could explore how the Jewish people overcame each hurdle of rebuilding the temple and city wall—which would be a wonderful study—I want to conclude by sharing the beautiful way God stirred the people's hearts after fifteen years of inactivity.

God raised up two prophets—Haggai and Zechariah—to speak to the people. And when these prophets framed the struggle from God's perspective, it gave the people courage to return to God's plan. Haggai said, "Thus says the LORD of hosts: These people say the time has not yet come to rebuild the house of the LORD. . . . 'Is it a time for you yourselves to dwell in your paneled houses, while this house lies in ruins? . . . Consider your ways'" (Hag. 1:2, 4–5).

Strong, isn't it? Apparently, when the temple work had stopped, the people redirected their energies from God's house to their personal lives, leaving the temple in ruins. Rather than centering their lives on God's purposes, they became discouraged by the opposition and then distracted by their pleasures and priorities. That'll preach.

And notice that God pinpointed the people's excuse for neglecting his house. They had said, "The time has not yet come." In other words, it wasn't a good time to serve in God's house.

Does this hit you like it does me? Is there an area of ministry where you've become discouraged and concluded it wasn't the right time?

Or has distraction crept in? Of course, we must be sensitive to our seasons of life, especially if we have small children. But if we are not careful, we can slip into thinking, *Not now*, when God might just be saying, "Now is the time."

The Promise We Can't Forget

This lesson has been meaningful to me because I often feel opposition when putting my hand to God's work. Even while working on this chapter, I sensed a strong opposition, an inner wrestling of my heart. Discouragement gripped me, creating a wall between me and God.

I kept trying to focus on God and *his* word to me. I kept trying to grasp what I know is true. But harassing thoughts muffled any sense of God's love or truth. Despite the negative narrative in my head, I kept reminding myself, *God, you are with me.* I'll be honest. I didn't feel him at the time, but the truth of his presence was the only thing I could think of to penetrate my wall of frustration.

It wasn't until the following day as I was rereading Haggai that God's truth solidified in my mind. When I saw how Haggai concluded his message to the discouraged people, I knew this was God's message for us: "Then Haggai, the messenger of the LORD, spoke to the people with the LORD's message, 'I am with you, declares the LORD'" (1:13).

I am with you. I couldn't believe it. This was the muffled whisper my soul longed to believe the day before.

God was not calling me to do things in my own strength or abilities. He wasn't "just a minute" away. Rather, he was there, calling me—as he is calling you—into a confident and joy-filled partnership of doing his work (John 15:5).

TRACING HIS PLAN THROUGH HISTORY

The Jewish people needed to hear the truth of God's abiding presence, and it's what you and I need to hear as well.

How did they respond to Haggai's message? When the people heard this message, "they came and worked on the house of the LORD" (1:14).

What a lesson for us! When the small group seems like too much work, when the ministry doesn't seem to be growing, when you are too exhausted to teach your children God's Word, when you wonder if your involvement makes a difference, when discouragement has turned into distraction, let this encouragement give you the confidence you need: God is with you.

Connection to Christ

Before we end today's study, let's consider the immense significance of these events. Cyrus's decree that moved God's people back to Jerusalem and to rebuild the temple was more than history—it was all part of God's bigger plan.

Remember, God had revealed that the Messiah would be born in Bethlehem (Mic. 5:2). By moving his people back to the land of promise, God was strategically moving them—and ultimately the Seed—to the prophesied location of the Messiah's birth.

More than that, Malachi, the final prophet of the Old Testament, would later prophecy, "And the Lord whom you seek will suddenly come to his temple; . . . he is coming" (Mal. 3:1).

Though the rebuilt temple was less splendid than Solomon's temple (Ezra 3:12), the glory of this temple would indeed surpass Solomon's because Jesus himself would fill it!

Truth and Trust

I love how today's lesson at the end of our journey through the Old Testament concludes where we began. God is with you. Jesus is in it all. Christ created all things, he is before all things, all things are for him, and he holds all things together (Col. 1:16–17). We've seen Christ as:

- Creator;
- the Seed promised to Abraham;
- the ram God provided in Isaac's place;
- Jacob's ladder connecting heaven to earth;
- the Passover Lamb freeing God's people from slavery;
- Ruth's kinsman-redeemer and protector;
- the Branch of Jesse;
- the Good Shepherd, Prince of Peace, and Suffering Servant;
- the One whose blood would inaugurate a new covenant; and
- the fourth man in the fiery furnace.

And for you and me, Christ is with us, scripting the story of our lives and drawing us close to him.

Remember, we don't have to be discouraged, controlled by the fear tactics of the Enemy or by our own insufficiencies. God is with us. His all-empowering presence can give us the confidence to walk forward, seeking the kingdom, living where we know his nearness, and recognizing Jesus in it all.

As we conclude our study of the Old Testament, we anticipate the New Testament, where we'll encounter the perfect fulfillment of God with us.

Jesus. Immanuel.

Questions

Have you ever set out to do something to demonstrate love for God or others, but you experienced more opposition than you expected?

How did you overcome the opposition?

Haggai noted the people had said it wasn't time to do God's work. Why is it important we recognize God's timing?

Is there a ministry or act of service you have been wanting to do but have become either discouraged or distracted in the process?

What steps will you take to step back into that ministry or act of service?

Haggai framed the question from God's perspective. Is there someone in your life who you look to for encouragement and who helps you reframe your situation from God's perspective?

Could you be that for someone else?

JESSE TREE

What is something you want to remember about the return to the land?

TRACING
HIS
Presence
IN OUR
LIVES

Day 22

MARY:
DELIVERING HIS MESSAGE

Read Luke 1:26–38.

We've come to the New Testament, and the promised Redeemer of Genesis 3:15 is born! Despite a flood, famine, family conflict, mass murders, wars, and exile, the promised Seed will come to inaugurate a new covenant. A covenant that is

- not based on law but on grace;
- not based on ritual but on relationship;

- not a formula, but forgiveness and friendship with the living God.

Through our deeds and efforts? Never. It's only by his gift of grace.

The news of a promised Redeemer first came to Adam and Eve in the garden and echoed to millions over time. And today we'll see what happened when the news of the Redeemer came to one teenage girl.[1] The virgin who God chose to give birth to the Promised One.

It was a personal encounter from a personal God. The same God who calls you and me.

A Personal Encounter

The angel Gabriel appeared to Mary and said:

> *Greetings, you who are highly favored! The Lord is with you. . . . Do not be afraid, Mary; you have found favor with God. You will conceive and give birth to a son, and you are to call him Jesus.* (Luke 1:28, 30–31 NIV)

I can only imagine the myriad questions and emotions that flooded the young virgin's mind. God was leading Mary into uncertain circumstances void of the details she longed to know. Yet the angel prefaced his announcement with a powerful promise, a truth that would sustain Mary through what the next nine months would entail: "The Lord is with you."

Think of how these words would have settled Mary's heart. Wherever life's path would lead, she could rest in the soul-soothing assurance that God was at her side.

Gabriel's message didn't end there. With the promise of God's pres-

Day 22 | Mary: Delivering His Message

ence, the angel also instructed Mary in how to rightly respond to God's presence and path for her: "Do not be afraid."

Even when everything in Mary wanted to fear, she could know she was not alone. She didn't need to be afraid or be overwhelmed by the unknown. She could cast herself on the promise of God's presence.

What thrills me about Gabriel's words is that this same promise applies to those who follow Jesus. In Hebrews, God said:

> *"Never will I leave you;*
> *never will I forsake you."*
>
> *So we say with confidence,*
>
> *"The Lord is my helper;*
> *I will not be afraid."*
> *(13:5–6 NIV)*

Don't miss this connection. In both Gabriel's message and the book of Hebrews, the promise of God's presence comes with the command or confession not to let fear control our lives.

My Insecurity, God's Sufficiency

I don't know if you're like me, but I need a reminder of his nearness. *Daily.* The other morning I awoke feeling completely buried by life. Commitments were mounting. Questions were swirling. I was anxious, insecure, and unsure how the day would go.

The kids were still asleep, so I went downstairs to pray. As I did, three biblical characters came to mind: Moses, Gideon, and Mary. At first the thought seemed random, but I quickly recalled a striking similarity in their stories: their own sense of fear and insecurity. To God's call, they each responded, "I don't have what it takes. It doesn't make sense."

Mary pleaded, "How will I give birth since I'm a virgin?"

Moses said, "Who am I to go to Pharaoh? I'm slow in speech."

Gideon asked, "How can I save Israel? I'm the weakest."

These questions—supported by perceived weakness—made Mary, Moses, and Gideon want to run away or question God's call.

Then I thought of another similarity in their stories. Not regarding their response to God but regarding God's promise to them: "I will be with you" (Judg. 6:16; Exod. 3:12; cf. Luke 1:28). And as much as I treasure God's promise of his presence, I also savor what God did not say. He didn't respond to their weaknesses with a list of their strengths. He didn't strike up a conversation about their Enneagram number or IQ. God said nothing of their ability. Rather, he assured them of something greater: his presence with them. A gift that would carry them through the challenges to come.

At that moment, I saw my own life in theirs—their weakness, questioning, and fear. More than that, God's response to their concerns gave me something on which to harness my heart that morning: The answer to my insecurity is never my sufficiency. The answer to my insecurity is his sufficiency. His presence with me.

Whatever is facing you today—big or small—would your burdens feel a little lighter with a gentle reminder that he is with you? Not just with Mary, Moses, or Gideon. Not just in the church service, small group, or devotion time. He's with you, even now.

Day 22 | Mary: Delivering His Message

A Fulfillment of Prophecy

Before we see Mary's response, I want us to notice a striking detail about Gabriel's announcement. Think back to the Davidic covenant and see if you hear a familiar echo in the angel's proclamation. "He [Jesus] will be great and will be called the Son of the Most High. And the Lord God will give to him the throne of his father David, and he will reign over the house of Jacob forever, and of his kingdom there will be no end" (Luke 1:32–33).

Do you see the connection? Gabriel proclaimed that God would give Jesus the throne of his father David. The references in Gabriel's message to Son, throne, David, reign, and forever all point to God's promise to David in 2 Samuel 7 (day 12).[2] Incredible!

Surrendered Response

As we end today, I want us to be encouraged by Mary's surrendered response to God's call. Let these words settle into your soul: "Behold, I am the servant of the Lord; let it be to me according to your word" (Luke 1:38). Despite the unknown, despite the fear, Mary found a place of rest in her heart—a place surrendered to the Father's plan. His will was her desire.

I love and long for that place, don't you? It's a place that doesn't insist on its own way, timing, or outcome. It's a place that says, "I'll do what you say. I'll surrender to your Word over me." It's a place that rests in the fact that God never leaves us and will work all things together for the good of those who love him (Rom. 8:28).

I'm convinced God calls us out of normalcy to embrace the invitation to follow Jesus. A path sometimes filled with questions, unexpected turns, and even heartbreaking events. Still, it is secured by the fact that he is with us.

God chose Mary to give birth to Jesus. And though we are not physically carrying the Christ child, God has given us the extreme honor of delivering his message to the world—a message of hope, love, salvation, and eternal life through him.

> Though we are not physically carrying the Christ child, God has given us the extreme honor of delivering his message to the world.

We see this in Jesus's words to his disciples. Read these words and let them speak directly to you. Read it aloud if you're comfortable. "You did not choose me, but I chose you and appointed you that you should go and bear fruit" (John 15:16).

Rest in this truth: Jesus has called you to know him, follow him, and bear fruit in this life. Perhaps your fruit is raising godly children or grandchildren, being a loving wife, serving in church, helping a friend, teaching, praying, witnessing in your workplace or school, or leading a Christ-centered business.

And here's what we must remember: The fruit-bearing abundance doesn't come from our striving and straining, people-pleasing, or living outside our limits or giftings. It comes as we abide under the wings of the One who invites us into a joy-filled relationship of trust.

As God guides us, he won't overwhelm us with the whole picture. He knows what to reveal and what not to reveal. He gently guides us with the next step, then the next. He wants us to live by faith and trust him in the process.

Truth and Trust

I pray that through our journey together, you are seeing that God is trustworthy. He is faithful to hear our prayers, provide strength through life's challenges, and bring us to his eternal dwelling when we pass from this life.

As we've walked through the Old Testament, we've watched God beautifully intersect the lives of ordinary men and women and exchange their brokenness for his blessing. I pray that seeing God in the lives of others has assured you of his presence in your own—that he has always been with you and always will be. Today in God's personal invitation to Mary, we've seen a woman who did not turn away in fear but confessed, "I am the servant of the Lord; let it be to me according to your word."

She believed.
She trusted.
She surrendered.
She followed.
Because she knew Immanuel, God with us.

May we have this same posture that surrenders, trusts, and rests in God's good plan for our life. It's a journey to know him more.

As we know him, we will trust him.

Questions

Take a moment to present yourself to God as his servant, prayerfully yielding your life to what he has for you. Take your time and be open to what he may be specifically speaking to you.

Mary presented herself as a servant to God. What would it look like for you to view yourself as God's servant?

How is it an honor to be God's servant?

List situations where you would benefit from hearing Jesus say, "I am with you." What difference does his presence make?

JESSE TREE

What is something you want to remember about Mary's response?

Day 23

SHEPHERDS:
FOLLOWING THE SAVIOR

Read Luke 2:1–20.

irth announcements. Wouldn't you say they've changed over the years? When Ryan and I found out we were expecting our first child, I made a few phone calls, and word got around.

But now we announce babies with social media posts, gender reveal parties, photo shoots, and more. And for good reason—having a baby is worth celebrating.

Despite the latest trends, nothing tops God's birth announcement for his only Son. Not only that, nothing shocked the world more than the surprising obscurity to whom the announcement would come—lowly shepherds in the field.

It's a magnificent story with a compelling and timeless message for you and me.

The Announcement

Bethlehem on the night of Jesus's birth would have bustled with out-of-town travelers who had come for Caesar's decreed registration. The town was so crowded that a young woman in her final hours of pregnancy would find herself staying in a stable.

Wouldn't you have loved to have been strolling through the dark fields of Bethlehem where shepherds watched their sheep? Perhaps they were talking and telling stories, or maybe they were rubbing their eyes from fatigue. Little did they know they were about to experience a moment they would never forget: "An angel of the Lord appeared to them, and the glory of the Lord shone around them, and they were filled with great fear" (Luke 2:9).

This stunning scene is one you likely know. But now, having traced Christ through the Old Testament, I think you'll find these familiar words fascinating: "Fear not, for behold, I bring you good news of great joy that will be for all the people. For unto you is born this day in the city of David a Savior, who is Christ the Lord" (vv. 10–11).

Before we go further, let's take in the profound significance of this announcement in light of what we've studied.

For all the people. Though Israel stood center stage in the Old Testament, the good news extended to *all* people. The gospel is for the Jew and Gentile, the shepherds and the saints, the nurse, teacher, architect, mail carrier, busy mom, and next-door neighbor. It's for the addict, the alcoholic, the incarcerated, and the one whose heart is hard toward God. The gospel is for all.

Born this day in the city of David. Through Micah's prophecy (day 18) we learned Bethlehem was the prophesied location of Jesus's birth. When the angel identified Bethlehem as the city of David, he was emphasizing the messianic role of Jesus.[1] Thousands of years earlier, God had promised David that the Messiah would come through his lineage (day 12, 2 Sam. 7). Jesus, born in David's city, would be the King who sits on David's throne (Luke 1:32). Incredible!

A Savior. Jesus wasn't merely a polished teacher, prophet, or moral activist. Jesus is the only one who saves people from their sins and redeems their lives from the curse (Matt. 1:21; Gal. 3:13). Jesus is the world's only way to salvation (Acts 4:12).

Who is Christ. We may think "Christ" is Jesus's last name. But "Christ" is the Greek translation of the word *messiah*, meaning "anointed one."[2] By calling the baby *Christ*, the angel identified Jesus as the prophesied Messiah! He was the promised Redeemer of Genesis 3:15 and the promised Seed of Abraham (Gen. 12:3; Gal. 3:16). He was the Mighty God and Prince of Peace (Isa. 9:6). He was the Branch of Jesse, the Good Shepherd, the Suffering Servant (Isa. 11:1; 40:11; 53). Jesus—the one who would fulfill thousands of years of prophecy and who the world longed to meet.

The Lord. Jesus was no ordinary baby. His conception was supernatural. He created all things and holds all things together (Col. 1:16–17). There is no one beside him or above him. He is Lord of all.

What an announcement! Savior, Christ, and Lord.

A Sign to the Shepherds

Following this extravagant announcement were instructions to the humblest place. "And this will be a sign for you: you will find a baby wrapped in swaddling cloths and lying in a manger" (Luke 2:12).

The shepherds didn't have to purify themselves and visit a palace, temple, or throne. Access to Jesus's presence didn't include a gated entry or sophisticated security. Rather, the shepherds would travel to a location familiar to their own—a keeping place for animals.

And this manger would be a *sign*.

Following the angel's announcement, the shepherds could have frantically searched house to house, trying to locate every baby boy in Bethlehem. But the angel narrowed their choices through the most unusual detail—a baby in a manger.

This detail both fascinates and encourages me. I'm sure the overbooked inn was inconvenient for Mary and Joseph, to put it nicely. But this inconvenience was the very sign God used to lead the shepherds to the Savior. It was God's will and God's sign.

Consider your own life. Have you ever thought your detours or delays could be God's design? Or have you seen God use delays or detours to place you or those you love where he wants?

The job opportunity that didn't work out, only to find a better fit.

The waiting list that made you choose a different school for your child.

The delayed answer to prayer that you now see was God's perfect timing.

The relationship you hoped would work out that you now know was not God's best.

Or perhaps you're experiencing an unusual delay or unexpected turn. Maybe you're in a low place of humility—a stable of sorts.

What if this series of delays, unusual paths, and humble places is God's way of placing you right where he wants you to be? And more beautifully, making you who he wants you to be. What if this place of waiting is teaching you to trust his timing, plan, heart, and care for you?

Wherever you are now, know that God could be using this season to prepare you for the next step. He has not forgotten you. Your detour is not a derailment. Your tangled path may just be the straight line of his will for you—a path to know him more (Acts 17:24–28).

The Messenger

Not only did the extravagant announcement lead to the lowliest location, but the angel delivered it to the humblest of people: shepherds.

Does this encourage you as it does me? Of all the people God could have chosen as the first to hear of Jesus's birth, he didn't select the ones with polished appearances, impressive portfolios, or a social media following. He didn't even choose a high-ranking official or the religious elite.

He spoke to those known for being lowly, outcasts, and sinful—those with no name.[3] He chose the one who has no name to bear his name.

He does the same today. God interrupts the lives of everyday people with an extraordinary invitation to follow him.

Truth and Trust

I think we savor the shepherds' story because we see ourselves in it. We live in the mundane, but God calls us to more. We live in the world, but God calls us not to be conformed to it. We live distracted and fragmented lives, but God calls us to follow him.

What compels me most about this story is *how* the shepherds went to see the baby: "They went with haste" (Luke 2:16). Can't you see the shepherds in their robes running to all the mangers they knew, eager to behold the Christ? I would have loved to have heard their conversations on the way and seen their eyes glisten through their dusty faces as they beheld the Savior for the first time. They went with haste—immediately and quickly, with a joy-filled expectancy, abandon, and delight.

> ### We live in the mundane, but God calls us to more.

I'm inspired by the response of the shepherds. Aren't you? As I read their reaction, I think, *What is my response when God nudges my heart? Do I ignore his call? Do I feel too busy? Distracted?*

We're good at hurrying and chasing after things. But the message that shines through this simple story is that God reaches ordinary people with an extraordinary and life-infusing invitation to follow him.

It's an invitation not to chase the world but to find a relationship with Jesus. It's a life marked not by straining and striving but by rest and relationship, a life not entangled in the traps of comparison but content in his plan.

It's the life Jesus offers you and me. It comes when we follow him.

The *Savior* of the world.
The promised *Christ.*
The *Lord* of all.

Questions

Which of the angel's proclamations of Jesus's identity speaks most significantly to you, and why?

- ☐ Savior (Savior of the world)
- ☐ Christ (the promised Messiah)
- ☐ Lord (Lord and master of all)

God reveals himself to ordinary people with an extraordinary message. Can you think of a time when you felt God revealed himself to you? For example, a church service, a Bible study, a conversation with a friend, a time of worship, with family?

If you were to describe the pace of your life, what would you say?

The shepherds went *with haste*. How could this be an example to you about following Jesus?

JESSE TREE

What is something you want to remember about the shepherds?

Day 24

WISE MEN:
REJOICING WITH GREAT JOY

Read Matthew 2.

In August 2017 a total solar eclipse displayed its beauty across the entire continental United States. America had not seen such a sight in nearly one hundred years.[1] Like a magnet, the eclipse compelled people to travel miles to watch. Crowds celebrated with T-shirts, banners, proposals, and even a wedding. The kids and I were glued to the TV all afternoon. Call me sappy, but tears flooded my eyes as we watched the special coverage.

The eclipse reminds me of another captivating event in the sky: a star that appeared more than two thousand years ago. It, too, compelled people to travel miles—not to watch a star but to worship a King.

Today we'll walk through Matthew 2 and explore the events surrounding this star. And because we're studying it through the lens of the promised Christ, we'll experience it with fresh meaning.

His Star

Matthew tells of the wise men's visit: "Now after Jesus was born in Bethlehem . . . wise men from the east came to Jerusalem, saying, 'Where is he who has been born king of the Jews? For we saw his star when it rose and have come to worship him'" (2:1–2).

We should remember the wise men were not a Christian men's group on a retreat or a weekend trip to the mountains. They were astrologers who traveled hundreds of miles—for likely one or two *years*—to worship a King.[2]

Notice how the star led the wise men to Jerusalem, not Bethlehem. Surprising, isn't it? Tuck that detail in your mind because we'll see more about the star's location as the story unfolds.

The wise men came to worship Jesus. All was well, right? While Christmas carols and nativity scenes may portray peace on earth, conflict was brewing. "When Herod the king heard this, he was troubled, and . . . he inquired of them where the Christ was to be born" (vv. 3–4). It's interesting to note that "King of the Jews" was a title Herod had received from the Roman senate.[3] I imagine when Herod heard the wise men speak of this new King, it bristled his flaming ego.

Herod asked where he could find Jesus. As you read the following verses, see if the chief priests' response to Herod's request reminds you of a previous day of study. They told him,

Day 24 | Wise Men: Rejoicing with Great Joy

In Bethlehem of Judea, for so it is written by the prophet:

"And you, O Bethlehem . . .
from you shall come a ruler
who will shepherd my people."
(vv. 5–6)

Don't you love how Scripture fits together? The religious leaders answered Herod's question with a seven-hundred-year-old prophecy—Micah 5:2, the same prophecy we covered on day 18.

Once Herod knew Jesus's location, he gave the wise men specific instructions: "Go and search diligently for the child, and when you have found him, bring me word, that I too may come and worship him" (v. 8).

I don't know about you, but Herod's words send a shiver down my spine. Though the request appears honorable, Herod was hiding his cold and cruel heart under a cloak of faith and religion.

The Star's Travel

Here's where the details surrounding the star become interesting. Remember from verse 1, the star led the wise men to Jerusalem, not Bethlehem. If the wise men followed Herod's command, they would presumably leave the star's location over Jerusalem and travel to Bethlehem.

With that in mind, let's watch what happened next: "Behold, the star that they had seen when it rose *went before them* until it came to *rest* over the place where the child was" (v. 9). Are you seeing this? The star, which had been over Jerusalem, went *before* the wise men and led them to Bethlehem, where it *rested* over the house where Jesus was.

For thousands of years, people have marveled over this star, suggesting it was the alignment of certain planets, a comet, or perhaps a super-nova. But think with me. Because of the earth's rotation, stars appear to travel east to west across the sky. But after the wise men left Jerusalem, the star went directly south (not west) to Bethlehem. Then it rested (stopped moving) where the wise men would find Jesus.[4] I'm no astronomer, but however this happened, it was a miraculous move of God.

In response, the wise men "rejoiced exceedingly with great joy. . . . They fell down and worshiped him" (vv. 10–11). Can you think of a more joyful phrase? They "rejoiced exceedingly with great joy." Worshiping and giving gifts. They were in the presence of the King.

A Surprising Provision

We know the wise men brought gold, frankincense, and myrrh to the child. And while these gifts may not have been the Binkies and baby wipes Mary hoped for, they were just what the couple needed. Because little did Mary and Joseph know what would happen next.

God warned Joseph in a dream: "Rise, take the child and his mother, and flee to Egypt, and remain there until I tell you, for Herod is about to search for the child, to destroy him" (v. 13). Enraged, Herod set out to destroy the Messiah.

But God had a different plan. In his perfect knowledge, God knew Mary and Joseph would need to escape Herod by traveling to Egypt.

Now, let's stop and consider the gifts. Many people comment on the gifts' symbolism, but what strikes me is their extreme practicality. These gifts, especially the gold, would have provided resources for the couple as they fled for their lives. God arranged the couple's funding by compelling astronomers living hundreds of miles away to give costly gifts.

This detail speaks to me deeply. God knows our needs, every potential resource, and every possible means to obtain it, in your situation and mine. Perhaps you are praying for God to provide something you need. Peace during a season of waiting. An open door of opportunity. Wisdom as you care for aging parents. Grace for a challenging relationship. Discernment as you raise your children.

Let this story stir your faith. God will do what it takes to provide in his way and his time. He loves us, knows all, and has no limits.

Herod's Plan

The tension builds in the story. Herod was pacing back and forth in Jerusalem, anxiously awaiting word from the wise men about Jesus's location. Meanwhile, Mary, Joseph, and Jesus were fleeing to Egypt for their lives.

But where were the wise men? "And being warned in a dream not to return to Herod, they departed to their own country by another way" (v. 12). I love this. God had told Joseph to travel to Egypt to escape Herod. And now, to add another layer of protection around Jesus, God told the wise men to avoid Herod by traveling a different way home. Amazing.

But the story isn't over. Once Herod realized he had been outwitted by the wise men, he "became furious, and he sent and killed all the male children in Bethlehem and in all that region who were two years old or under" (v. 16).

What a devastating act.

Let's stop to consider what was happening in the bigger salvation story. Jesus was not any child. He was God in the flesh—the promised Seed—whose life would crush the head of the Serpent, bringing salvation for all who believe (Gen. 3:15; John 3:16).

What if Herod's actions stemmed not only from his brash ego but were an extension of the Enemy's hand, attempting to destroy the Seed through whom the world would be blessed?

And yet, despite the Enemy's schemes, how much greater is God's hand and plan:

- He set his star in the heavens as an invitation for wise men to worship Jesus.
- The wise men gave gifts that funded the family's escape.
- To protect Jesus, God told Joseph to find refuge in Egypt.
- To prevent the wise men from telling Herod about Jesus's location, God warned them to go home another way.

It's a lesson we can hold close to our hearts. God has a perspective we don't have. He loves us and is at work behind the scenes, orchestrating the events of our lives to accomplish his divine purpose. Even when the Enemy attempts to derail us from God's plan, we can know God has a better way. Always.

It requires us to lean into him, follow his path, and listen for his directives.

Truth and Trust

The wise men have left us an example to follow. These men

- obeyed the promptings of God;
- sacrificially followed him;

- gave generous gifts;
- responded to God's presence with joy; and
- worshiped the Creator, not the creation.

It's easy to read a list like this and miss the specific way God may be speaking to us. Would you join me in reviewing this list and prayerfully choosing one area you feel God may be nudging you to follow him more closely?

For example, you might want to be less distracted and more responsive to God's promptings. Perhaps you long to know the joy of God's presence in your everyday life. Maybe you sense he is calling you to be more generous. Or perhaps you often focus on created things—looks, possessions, influencers—and you know he is drawing you to focus on him.

Remember this—*exceedingly great joy* comes from following and worshiping the Savior. The One who holds every star in place, provides for our needs, and orchestrates our lives to further his divine plan.

As I think back to the solar eclipse of 2017, I remember America's response: cheers, travel, and celebration. At the same time, my heart grieved because I thought, *The world is missing it. They're focused on the creation and missing their Creator!*

The beauty of today's story is this:

> The wise men sought the Savior, not the star.
> They came to worship, not watch.
> Their priority was the Creator, not the creation.

To the wise men, God used a brilliant display of celestial beauty to invite them to follow him. And to you and me, he's given the Light of the World—Jesus—who invites us to follow him. It's the life and love the world craves, and it brings a joy that exceeds the best the world can offer. It happens as we follow and worship him.

Questions

Has there been a time in your life when you've seen God provide in a way you did not expect or in a way you knew was his doing?

Is there a situation where you currently need his provision?

Of all the ways the wise men responded to the Savior, which one speaks most significantly to you?

☐ Obeying the promptings of God.
☐ Sacrificially following him.
☐ Giving generous gifts.
☐ Responding to God's presence with joy.
☐ Worshiping the Creator, not the creation.

In what specific ways do you sense God leading you?

JESSE TREE

What is something you want to remember about the wise men?

Day 25

LIVING IN THE LIGHT OF JESUS

Read John 8:12; 1 Peter 5:6–10.

It was the morning of my wedding. As I opened the church doors and entered the dimly lit foyer, a woman approached me to share news no bride expects to hear. "You won't believe this. We just lost power!" she said.

"It's fine," I squeaked, trying to keep calm. "I'm sure it will come on in a few minutes."

One hour went by. Then another. Those "few minutes" became an entire day *and* wedding without electricity. Let's just say that put a little kink in the plan. We had no power for microphones, stage lights, or prerecorded music. There were no studio lights for the photographer or any lights in the bathroom. We had no power for curling irons, and there was no heat in the building for a winter wedding in West Virginia.

Good thing I was so relaxed to begin with. *Not really.*

I'll be honest—it wasn't all bad. In place of prerecorded music, a friend played his guitar. Instead of lights in the sanctuary, we enjoyed natural light from skylights and warm lights from the candelabra. Apart from me looking uncomfortable in the photos because I was shivering, the wedding was a success.

In our world of modern conveniences, it's easy to overlook the importance of light because we're rarely without it. It's only in situations when the electricity goes out at night (or on your wedding day) that we stumble, stub our toes, and eagerly await the return of something upon which we depend so heavily.

But in the ancient culture of the Bible, light was valued differently. Without the ease of electricity, people knew the presence of only one light changed everything. And into that ancient setting, the prophet Isaiah spoke of such a Light—not a physical light, but something far greater:

> *The people who walk in darkness*
> *will see a great light.*

TRACING HIS PRESENCE IN OUR LIVES

For those who live in a land of deep darkness,
a light will shine.

(Isa. 9:2 NLT)

A light will shine. Through our study of the Old Testament, we've seen men like Isaiah, Jeremiah, Nathan, Ezekiel, and Micah prophesy of a coming hope. These and other men spoke messianic prophecies, which continued through the time of Malachi (around 450 BC).

After Malachi, a pivot occurred. Rather than receiving prophecies of hope, the world endured four hundred years of spiritual silence. No words from God. No hope-filled prophecies. Instead, there was persecution. Oppression. Waning hope.

But as Isaiah had prophesied, those who walked in darkness would see a great light. Seven hundred years after Isaiah's prophecy, the cry of a newborn babe broke the silence and illuminated the world. The Light had come!

Day 25 | Living in the Light of Jesus

Men, full of the spirit, recognized Jesus as the Light:

- Simeon said Jesus was "a light for revelation to the Gentiles" (Luke 2:32).
- John wrote Jesus was the "true light" (John 1:9).
- Matthew even quoted Isaiah, saying Jesus was "a great light" (Matt. 4:16).

Jesus was the one true Light who would dispel the darkness and bring the light of eternal life to all who believe. And of all the verses concerning light, none speaks more profoundly and personally than the words of Jesus himself: "I am the light of the world. Whoever follows me will not walk in darkness, but will have the light of life" (John 8:12).

On our final day together, we'll unpack this compelling statement to see Jesus as the Light of the World and the Light of our lives.

The Backdrop

When Jesus announced he was the Light of the World, it was no small moment. To understand its profound significance, I'll explain the setting—the Feast of Tabernacles. This feast was an annual Jewish celebration when people remembered the forty years God had cared for their ancestors in the wilderness. During these forty years, the people lived in "tabernacles"—or tents—and God supernaturally led them with a pillar of cloud by day and a pillar of fire by night.

During the Feast of Tabernacles, four massive candelabras blazed in the temple's court, illuminating the entire city. These iconic lights reminded people of the pillar of fire in the wilderness.[1]

Picture the scene. In the temple court, people danced, sang, and remembered the light that had guided their ancestors. They did all this under the light of the stunning candelabras.

Then entered Jesus, proclaiming, "I am the light."

Don't miss this beautiful connection. More than a thousand years earlier, the Jewish people had followed God's presence in the pillar of fire. And then at the Feast of Tabernacles—a time remembering that light—Jesus said, "I am the light." Not only for the wilderness but for the world. Incredible.

Following the Light

One of the most important words of Jesus's statement is one we easily overlook—*follow*: "I am the light of the world. Whoever follows me will not walk in darkness, but will have the light of life" (John 8:12).

When the children of Israel were in the wilderness, the pillar of fire provided light in the darkness and warmth on the cool desert nights. It was more than a stunning sight to behold. It was the Lord going before them, providing his loving guidance and protection (Exod. 13:21). The light was there to be followed.

In the same way, when Jesus came from heaven to earth, he was more than a stunning sight to behold. He came to be followed. And this word *follow* makes all the difference.

Think of how foolish it would have been for the children of Israel to marvel at the light and then ignore its lead. Or say, "How miraculous!" and then trek the other way. If we're not careful, we may do something similar. We may *see* the Light but not *seek* the Light. We may *admire* Jesus without *following* Jesus.

To the Jews at the Feast of Tabernacles and to you and me, Jesus does not present himself as some*thing* to only be admired; he is some*one* to follow. Why is this so important? Jesus continues: "Whoever follows me will not walk in darkness, but will have the light of life" (John 8:12).

Day 25 | Living in the Light of Jesus

> We may see the Light but not
> seek the Light. We may admire
> Jesus without following Jesus.

Growing up I watched a show called *Ripley's Believe It or Not!*, which showcased unusual people doing extraordinary things. In one episode a man shared his story of eating an entire bicycle. Wheels, tires, gears, spokes. You name it. He ate it. Believe it or not.

How was this possible? The man diced the bicycle into minuscule pieces, and over time he consumed it bit by bit, piece by piece.

Here's what strikes me. This man's story tells me that we will ingest and digest *anything*. As long as it's given to us in small enough pieces.

The Enemy knows this. He'll feed us little lie after little lie—bit by bit, piece by piece—until we've ingested the whole dark truth that distorts the goodness of God and our value in this world.

If we continue to ingest these lies, they mound into the darkness of discouragement, depression, doubt, and addiction. In our relationships, we may experience the darkness of anger, unforgiveness, division, and bitterness. If we don't expose and overcome this darkness with God's light, we'll live in defeat rather than joy and peace.

But Jesus promises a better way—a relationship of living in his light.

Truth and Trust

As I've listened to women's stories over the years and walked through my own struggles, I've discovered the direction of our life hinges on whether we live by lies or cling to truth, whether we follow our own desires or follow Jesus. When we feel ourselves getting frazzled, upset, or discouraged, we need to step out of the chaos and connect with God.

This could take three minutes or thirty minutes. In these moments we remind ourselves of what is true and what is a lie. Of who we are and *whose* we are. Of what is God's voice and what is the Enemy's deception. We remind ourselves of what matters most—loving him and those around us. And then with this connection and renewed perspective, we reenter the rhythm of our day, following the Light of life.

Here's what the Enemy does not want you to know. You don't have to live in his dark path of destruction. A life of love and peace is God's plan. In fact, it is his promise to us: "Whoever follows me . . . will have the light of *life*" (John 8:12).

We will have life! Not just a pulse but a purpose. Jesus promises a life that is peaceful, joy-filled, and free! This is what we crave, what we were made for, and what Jesus promises.

God never intended us to live in the darkness of defeat. He never intended us to scratch our heads, wondering if he cares or is there. He desires us to know the richness of a relationship with him, the power of the Spirit, the joy of worship, and the freedom truth brings (Ps. 16:11; 34:8; John 8:32).

He invites us to follow him. Do you hunger for this like me?

The path before us is one of simple surrender to God's plan. In the words of the apostle Paul, it's forgetting what is behind and pressing toward what is ahead (Phil. 3:13–14). It's when we confess, "I am the servant of the Lord; let it be to me according to your word" (Luke 1:38).

It's not just a dream. It's the life Jesus promises as we follow him.

The Light of the World.
The Beginning and the End.
The Author of our salvation.
The Seed of Abraham.
The Son of David.
The Lamb of God.
The Prince of Peace.
The Mediator of a new covenant.
The One who is Jesus.
God with us.

Questions

How has our journey through the Scripture expanded your understanding of Jesus?

How does this bigger view of Jesus affect your faith?

How does Jesus's invitation to "follow me" speak specifically to you?

What practical steps will you take toward admiring *and* following Jesus?

JESSE TREE

What is something you want to remember about the Light of the World?

ACKNOWLEDGMENTS

This book represents the fruit of decades of faithful men and women, teachers, seminary professors, pastors, Sunday school teachers, and friends pouring into my life and pointing me to Jesus. From Bill Hampton, who knocked on our family's door and shared the gospel when I was four years old, to our current pastor, Brandon Samuel, whose grace-filled messages bring life to my family's hearts every Sunday.

My biggest thanks goes to my husband and best friend, Ryan. Thank you for your support, love, laughter, and sweet willingness to hear *another* new creative idea over breakfast. You are God's gift to me.

Thank you to my daughter, Charity, for providing illustrations and devoting countless hours of edits, invaluable input, and rich conversations. Thank you to my son, Isaiah, for your constant encouragement, love for Jesus, quick wit, and sweet hugs that make my heart sing.

I'm deeply grateful to my precious mom and dad, who have selflessly poured their love into me, given me courage, and helped me follow my dream.

Special thanks to Anna Holzbach, who has been a faithful friend, ministry partner, and voice of wisdom and love through years of Bible studies and this project. Thank you to the Read Team for their edits,

ACKNOWLEDGMENTS

creative ideas, laughs, smiling faces, and nighttime Zoom calls. Thank you to Melanie Chitwood for helping me frame my ideas and providing accountability and invaluable insight.

Thank you to Back to the Bible for your ongoing friendship and partnership in ministry. It is such a joy to be a part of the team.

A heartfelt thanks to my agent, Blythe Daniel, who saw the book's potential from the beginning and has served as both a huge advocate and an invaluable source of wisdom.

A big thank-you goes to Kregel Publications for embracing the book's vision, hearing my heart, and being a delight to work with from the beginning. Thank you to my developmental editor, Dori Harrell, for making the book blossom through Spirit-led guidance and a commitment to truth. Thank you to Wendy Widder Huisken for assuring biblical integrity and clarity. And to Rachel Kirsch and Kayliani Shi, thank you for your attentiveness, wisdom, and kind hearts.

One of the most vital groups to thank is those who have prayed for me throughout this project. My childhood bestie and forever friend, Kellie Snuffer, stands on the front line. The Spirit-filled prayers of these men and women sustained and strengthened me to complete something that many days seemed impossible.

Finally and most passionately, all praise, thanks, and glory go to Jesus Christ, my Savior, Lord, and closest friend.

APPENDIX A

Making the Jesse Tree Part of Your Christmas Tradition

I want to ask a few questions that may probe (just a bit) into your feelings about the holidays. Take a moment to answer these questions honestly.

During the holidays . . .

- Do you often feel behind or like what you're doing is not enough?
- Do your stress levels soar, making it difficult to enjoy the season?
- Do strained family relationships complicate family gatherings?
- Do you face reminders of loss, either of a loved one or the struggle of an ongoing situation?
- Do you wish your family focused less on gifts and more on Jesus?

These questions can make us realize how easily we can become rundown by the holidays. Though Christmas should be associated with joy, it is often marked by stress, anxiety, and depression. The busyness and demands of the season pull our hearts away from the Savior.

APPENDIX A

That's what I love about the Jesse Tree.

The Jesse Tree provides families or individuals of any life stage or age an opportunity to refocus their hearts on the true meaning of Christmas during the entire month of December.

How Does It Work?
Each of the twenty-five stories we covered in our study has a corresponding Christmas ornament representing that specific story (see "Where Do I Get the Ornaments?"). During each day in December leading up to Christmas, add one ornament to a decorative tree in your home, beginning with day 1 from our study. By Christmas Day you will have traced the promise of Christ through the Old Testament. (See appendix E for "The Jesse Tree Ornament Chart.")

What Kind of Tree Do I Use?
Anything works. We use a smaller tree (about two feet tall) for the Jesse Tree ornaments. This has been my favorite way, as guests often ask us to explain the tree's meaning. I have seen other families display the ornaments on wreaths, metal ornament trees, or with their primary Christmas tree.

What Do I Do Each Day?
Add that day's ornament to your tree. This can be as simple or involved as you like. If you are adding the ornaments on your own, you could review or reread that chapter in the book. If you are adding the ornaments as a family, you could tell the story in a few words or read it in the Bible.

There is no need to stress with details. I've found it best to keep it short and fun. Since this is something you can do every year, don't feel the burden to cover every aspect.

Where Do I Get the Ornaments?

You can create your own or search online for a collection to purchase. On my website, which you can access at the QR code below, I offer a free printable set of illustrations you can use to make your own ornaments. Check out appendix C, "Quick Tips for a Successful Ornament Exchange," for an idea on how to collaborate with others to create a set of ornaments. Be creative and have fun!

APPENDIX B

The Origin of the Jesse Tree

The Jesse Tree is a visual illustration of the promised Christ in the Old Testament. Dating back to the Middle Ages, this ancient picture would appear in religious art, such as stained-glass windows and paintings.[1] We see current examples of the Jesse Tree in Chartres Cathedral in France and Westminster Abbey in London. These visual representations allowed people of all ages to grasp Jesus's lineage and the beauty of God's plan to send a Savior.

The name originates from an Old Testament prophecy we covered on day 14. It's Isaiah's prophecy stating that a Branch would come from Jesse, King David's father. "There shall come forth a shoot from the stump of Jesse, and a branch from his roots shall bear fruit" (Isa. 11:1).

We can think of the Jesse Tree like a family tree. Traditionally, Jesse (David's father) would be at the base of the tree, with his descendants and symbols springing up on layers of foliage, reaching up to the Branch, who is Jesus.[2]

APPENDIX C

Quick Tips for a Successful Ornament Exchange

If you're reading *Tracing His Promise* as part of a book club or Bible study, an ornament exchange is a perfect way to conclude the study. After weeks of being together, it is fun for members to express themselves through the ornament they choose to make.

Think of it like a cookie exchange, where each person makes a certain number of ornaments to trade with others. For example, I once made scrolls representing Josiah. At the exchange, everyone brought homemade ornaments. Each person walked away with a complete set of twenty-five ornaments corresponding to the twenty-five stories of the Jesse Tree.

Here are a few tips for a successful exchange:

- **Have sign-ups:** At one of the first few meetings, share about the exchange and pass around a sheet for people to choose the ornament(s) they would like to make. Visit www.donnaamidon.org /tracinghispromise for a printable sign-up sheet.

- **Choose your exchange date:** It works well to do the exchange near the end of the study or even to make it part of the last day. If you are doing a fall group, be sure your exchange happens before December 1.

- **Make the ornaments:** The ornaments can be as elaborate or as simple as each person likes. Clear plastic ornament bulbs are a great start. You can find fun ideas online by searching "Jesse Tree Ornaments."

- **Determine the number of ornaments:** Each participant makes the same number of ornaments as there are people in the group. For example, if twenty people are in the group and someone signed up to make a globe, that person would make twenty globes.

  - **Smaller groups:** Remember, each ornament needs a name assigned to it. For smaller groups, this means everyone makes two or three different kinds of ornaments. For example, if there are seven people in the group and someone signs up to make Joseph's coat, Noah's ark, and Josiah's scroll, then on the day of the exchange, that person brings seven ornaments of Joseph's coat, seven of Noah's ark, and seven of Josiah's scroll.

  - **Larger groups:** For groups of more than twenty-five, not everyone will need to make an ornament. But always remember to make enough ornaments so everyone has a set when the exchange is over.

- **Bring two boxes to the exchange:** Bring one box with the ornaments you've made and one empty box (labeled with your name) to receive your ornaments in. Helpful hint: a week or two before the exchange, take the first part of the meeting to confirm that everyone knows what ornament they will be making so there are no surprises on the exchange day.

On the day of the exchange:

- **Have each person introduce their ornament:** They can also explain how they made their ornaments and share any fun fact or fail they had along the way. Some women have told stories about their husbands or children joining in. Other people have shared moving stories about what made them choose that particular ornament. It's a fun way for group members to connect. Plus, it makes the ornaments more meaningful.

- **Exchange the ornaments:** I typically have group members place their empty boxes along an open wall or long table. Then everyone walks through and places one of their ornaments in each box. It's like walking through a buffet line, but rather than putting food on your plate, you place one ornament in each box.

- **Double-check before you leave:** After the exchange, it is helpful to review the list of twenty-five ornaments one final time, ensuring everyone has one of each ornament. This will save you texts and phone calls later. Believe me.

You're all set! Have fun and make memories!

APPENDIX D

Peace and Confidence Through Praying God's Promises

God has given us his Word as a weapon to overcome the opposition we face (Matt. 4:1–13; Eph. 6:17–18). Following are some of my favorite verses and promises to pray, beginning with one I like to pray for my children.

Prayer for Others

We have not ceased to pray for you, asking that you may be filled with the knowledge of his will in all spiritual wisdom and understanding, so as to walk in a manner worthy of the Lord, fully pleasing to him: bearing fruit in every good work and increasing in the knowledge of God; being strengthened with all power, according to his glorious might, for all endurance and patience with joy. (Col. 1:9–11)

I pray for my children _____(names), asking that they would be filled with the knowledge of your will in all spiritual wisdom and understanding. I pray they would walk in a manner worthy of you, fully pleasing to you, bearing fruit in every good work, and increasing in the knowledge of who you are. Today, I ask that their hearts would stay tender toward you. May they walk in the strength of your mighty hand and presence in their life.

Confidence and Trust
And those who know your name put their trust in you,
for you, O LORD, have not forsaken those who seek you.
(Ps. 9:10)

Thank you that as I know you, I will trust you. Open the eyes of my understanding. Speak to me through your Word. May I have a spirit of wisdom and revelation in the knowledge of you. May I comprehend the depth of your love for me and for others. May I walk in faith and belief for things only you can do.

Walking in God's Strength
His divine power has given us everything we need for a godly life
through our knowledge of him who called us. (2 Peter 1:3 NIV)

Thank you that even when I feel weak, your divine power has given me everything I need for a godly life. You have given me what I need to work my job, raise my kids, love my spouse, love others in your name, and do what you have put before me to do. I pray I may know and walk in your power regarding_____.

Boldness in Prayer
Let us then with confidence draw near to the throne of grace,
that we may receive mercy and find grace to help in time of
need. (Heb. 4:16)

Thank you that I can come boldly to your throne of grace in this time of need. The boldness is from nothing I have done. It is all a gift of your grace. It was your covenant, your grace, your blood, your sacrifice, and the veil that you tore in two that grants me the freedom to come with confidence. And so I come boldly, not timidly, and bring these requests to you: _____.

Effective Prayer

And this is the confidence that we have toward him, that if we ask anything according to his will he hears us. And if we know that he hears us in whatever we ask, we know that we have the requests that we have asked of him. (1 John 5:14–15)

Father, thank you that when I ask anything according to your will, you hear me. You are not far, your ear is not deaf, and your hand is not short. Guide me and give me wisdom even now, that I may ask things that align with your will. Today, I ask for _____.

God's Will Working in Us

And I am sure of this, that he who began a good work in you will bring it to completion at the day of Jesus Christ. (Phil. 1:6)

Thank you for promising to complete the good work you began in my life. Even when I feel discouraged by challenging days and unexpected setbacks, I thank you that you are working. You have not stopped working and will complete what you began in my life and in the lives of those I love.

Fruit-Filled Living

I am the vine; you are the branches. Whoever abides in me and I in him, he it is that bears much fruit, for apart from me you can do nothing. (John 15:5)

Thank you that as I abide in you, I will bear fruit. May I know that place of connection—a place not pulled by distraction or the allures of this world. May I stay close to your heart today and produce abundant and beautiful fruit glorifying you.

Wisdom

If any of you lacks wisdom, let him ask God, who gives generously to all without reproach, and it will be given him. (James 1:5)

Thank you for promising your wisdom to those who ask. May I not doubt but stay steady and secure in you. Thank you for promising to give generously and without finding fault. Let me discern your directives and have the courage and faith to obey. I ask for wisdom specifically for_____.

God's Provision

Ask, and it will be given to you; seek, and you will find; knock, and it will be opened to you. (Matt. 7:7)

I thank you for the promise that when I ask, it will be given. When I seek, I will find. And when I knock, the door will be opened. I will not sit in passivity but rather press into you and ask for your touch, power, and favor on these areas of my life—for your glory.

Trusting His Plan

And we know that for those who love God all things work together for good, for those who are called according to his purpose. (Rom. 8:28)

Father, I thank you that everything in my life—even the tangled web of my situation—will work out for good. May I have faith to believe in your goodness even during challenging times and during the days that make me want to quit. May I walk in your purpose and divine plan.

Strength for Hard Times

He said to me, "My grace is sufficient for you, for my power is made perfect in weakness." Therefore I will boast all the more gladly of my weaknesses, so that the power of Christ may rest upon me. For the sake of Christ, then, I am content with weaknesses, insults, hardships, persecutions, and calamities. For when I am weak, then I am strong. (2 Cor. 12:9–10)

In times of weakness and hardship, I pray your strength would shine through. Give me wisdom as I move forward through this day. Strength to work at my job. Strength to love my family, care for myself well, and be a witness for you. May others see your strength in me as I walk through testing times with grace and confidence. I recognize my weakness, yet like Paul, I rejoice because it is in your strength that I want to live.

Resting in God's Love

For I am sure that neither death nor life, nor angels nor rulers, nor things present nor things to come, nor powers, nor height nor depth, nor anything else in all creation, will be able to separate us from the love of God in Christ Jesus our Lord. (Rom. 8:38–39)

Though hard times make me question your love and kindness, I thank you that what I'm facing today has not separated me from your love. May my mind and heart have eyes to see that I am loved by you. May my soul settle because it is embraced by you.

Forgiveness

If we confess our sins, he is faithful and just to forgive us our sins and to cleanse us from all unrighteousness. (1 John 1:9)

Father, I confess that I so often push you aside, become distracted by the world's allurements, disobey your Word, and resist the Spirit's leading. Thank you that I can come to you, receive forgiveness, and be cleansed from all unrighteousness. I confess and ask you to forgive me of _____. Thank you for the sacrifice of Jesus and the gift of forgiveness and freedom from condemnation, guilt, and shame.

Forgiving Others

Be kind to one another, tenderhearted, forgiving one another, as God in Christ forgave you. (Eph. 4:32)

That person who offended, betrayed, hurt, disappointed, or falsely accused me, I choose to forgive. Father, you see my hurt and how challenging this is. I pray for healing from the way their actions have hurt or harmed me. I pray I can use this challenging time as a way to love and empathize with others. I release the right to retaliate, seek revenge, or gossip. Though I may still feel disappointed and wounded, I make the decision to forgive and pray for the ability to walk free from the burden of bitterness and unforgiveness. Rather than take things in my own hands, I humble myself and forgive, just as you, in Christ Jesus, have forgiven me.

Salvation of Others

Even if our gospel is veiled, it is veiled to those who are perishing. The god of this age has blinded the minds of unbelievers, so that they cannot see the light of the gospel that displays the glory of Christ, who is the image of God. (2 Cor. 4:3–4 NIV)

Father, I pray for the salvation of _____. I ask that you would remove the blinders on their eyes so they can see the glorious light of the gospel and come to a saving knowledge of you. I pray you would send people with the message of Jesus into the lives of my family and friends who don't know you. I ask you would let these laborers talk about you with love and in a way that connects and speaks to the

APPENDIX D

hearts of those listening. Anoint them and give them boldness to plant seeds that will produce the fruit of knowing you. And give me the boldness and courage to be the answer to someone's prayer for the salvation of someone I know. May I shine your light, connect with others, and always be ready to give an answer for the hope I have.

Overcoming Fear
For God has not given us a spirit of fear, but of power and of love and of a sound mind. (2 Tim. 1:7 NKJV)

In whatever I face today, you have promised me power, love, and a sound mind. Even though my heart wants to fear, I choose to trust in you. I will not fear what's before me. I will not be overwhelmed by the anxiety or fear of what I currently face or anticipate. I cast myself upon your strength. May I know your limitless power, be compelled and controlled by your love, and have a mind that is sound, solid, and at peace.

Peace of Mind
You keep him in perfect peace
whose mind is stayed on you,
because he trusts in you.
(Isa. 26:3)

When my mind floods with fears, concerns, and fatigue, thank you for the promise of perfect peace. May my mind stay on you and trust in you. I pray that my mind would not be swayed by circumstance, troubled by trials, or discouraged by doubt. Give me the grace to set my mind on you today and to trust you completely.

Peace Through Prayer
Do not be anxious about anything, but in everything by prayer and supplication with thanksgiving let your requests be made known to God. And the peace of God, which sur-

passes all understanding, will guard your hearts and your minds in Christ Jesus. (Phil. 4:6-7)

Father, thank you that anxiety and worry do not have to define me, control me, or confuse me. Thank you that when I bring my requests before you, with thanksgiving, I can rest because I know these situations are under your divine and loving care. Today I bring to you these requests: _____.

APPENDIX E

The Jesse Tree Ornament Chart

Day	Chapter Title	Ornament
1	Christ in Creation	Globe Ornament
2	Man's Sin, God's Promise	Apple/Snake Ornament
3	Noah: Walking with God	Noah's Ark Ornament
4	Abraham: When God Promises the Impossible	Abraham Ornament
5	Issac: Do You Trust Me?	Ram Ornament
6	Jacob: You're Never Alone	Ladder Ornament
7	Joseph: God Meant It for Good	Joseph's Coat Ornament
8	Passover: Divine Deliverance	Doorframe Ornament
9	The Law: What We Could Never Do	Two Tablets of Stone Ornament
10	Joshua: Faith over Feeling	Grapes Ornament
11	Ruth: Refuge in the Kinsman-Redeemer	Wheat Ornament
12	David: When Life Takes a Turn	Crown Ornament
13	Josiah: Life in Dry Seasons	Scroll Ornament

The Jesse Tree Ornament Chart

14	Jesse Tree: Your Story Isn't Over	Tree Stump Ornament
15	He Is Our Peace	Dove Ornament
16	He Is My Shepherd	Shepherd/Sheep Ornament
17	He Will Suffer for Me	Cross Ornament
18	Bethlehem: God Is in the Details	Bethlehem Ornament
19	New Covenant: Change Is Coming	Heart Ornament
20	Exile: The Fourth Man in the Fire	Fiery Furnace Ornament
21	Return from Exile: Strength for God's Work	Wall Ornament
22	Mary: Delivering His Message	Manger Ornament
23	Shepherds: Following the Savior	Angels Ornament
24	Wise Men: Rejoicing with Great Joy	Star Ornament
25	Living in the Light of Jesus	Light of the World Ornament

NOTES

Day 1 | *Christ in Creation*

1. The doctrine of the Trinity is a teaching central to Christianity: there is one God who exists as three eternal, coexistent persons (Father, Son, and Spirit).
2. Pat Brennan, "What in the World Is an 'Exoplanet?'," NASA Exoplanet Exploration, April 12, 2018, https://exoplanets.nasa.gov/news/1499/what-in-the -world-is-an-exoplanet.
3. Brennan, "What in the World Is an 'Exoplanet?'"
4. "Constant Speed," American Museum of Natural History, accessed January 24, 2024, https://www.amnh.org/exhibitions/einstein/light/constant-speed.
5. Elizabeth Howell and Ailsa Harvey, "How Many Galaxies Are There?," Space .com, February 1, 2022, https://www.space.com/25303-how-many-galaxies -are-in-the-universe.html.
6. Brennan, "What in the World Is an 'Exoplanet?'"

Day 2 | *Man's Sin, God's Promise*

1. Allen P. Ross, "Genesis," in *The Bible Knowledge Commentary: An Exposition of the Scriptures*, ed. J. F. Walvoord and R. B. Zuck, vol. 1 (Wheaton, IL: Victor Books, 1985), 33.
2. Douglas Mangum, *The Lexham Glossary of Theology* (Bellingham, WA: Lexham, 2014), s.v. "protoevangelium."
3. James 4:7; Ephesians 6:13–14; 1 Thessalonians 5:17.

Day 3 | *Noah: Walking with God*

1. K. A. Mathews, *Genesis 1–11:26*, New American Commentary 1A (Nashville: Broadman & Holman, 1996), 364.

NOTES

2. Noah may not have harvested every tree himself. However, he was responsible for making sure every needed tree was harvested.

3. Allen P. Ross, "Genesis," in *The Bible Knowledge Commentary: An Exposition of the Scriptures*, ed. J. F. Walvoord and R. B. Zuck, vol. 1 (Wheaton, IL: Victor Books, 1985), 38.

Day 4 | *Abraham: When God Promises the Impossible*

1. David Limbaugh, *The Emmaus Code: Finding Jesus in the Old Testament* (Washington, DC: Regnery, 2015), 97.

2. Donald K. Campbell, "Galatians," in *The Bible Knowledge Commentary: An Exposition of the Scriptures*, ed. J. F. Walvoord and R. B. Zuck, vol. 2 (Wheaton, IL: Victor Books, 1985), 598.

3. Kurt Strassner, *Opening up Genesis*, Opening Up Commentary (Leominster, England: Day One, 2009), 60–61.

4. K. A. Mathews, *Genesis 11:27–50:26*, New American Commentary 1B (Nashville: Broadman & Holman, 2005), 171–72.

5. Mathews, *Genesis*, 175.

Day 6 | *Jacob: You're Never Alone*

1. James M. Freeman and Harold J. Chadwick, *Manners & Customs of the Bible* (North Brunswick, NJ: Bridge-Logos Publishers, 1998), 49. The term "ministering spirits" comes from Hebrews 1:14.

Day 7 | *Joseph: God Meant It for Good*

1. Genesis 42:24; 43:30; 45:2, 14–15; 46:29; 50:1; 50:17.

Day 8 | *Passover: Divine Deliverance*

1. John D. Hannah, "Exodus," in *The Bible Knowledge Commentary: An Exposition of the Scriptures*, ed. J. F. Walvoord and R. B. Zuck, vol. 1 (Wheaton, IL: Victor Books, 1985), 129.

Day 9 | *The Law: What We Could Never Do*

1. James E. Smith, *The Pentateuch*, 2nd ed., Old Testament Survey Series (Joplin, MO: College Press, 1993), 299.

NOTES

Day 10 | Joshua: Faith over Feeling

1. Eugene H. Merrill, "Numbers," in *The Bible Knowledge Commentary: An Exposition of the Scriptures*, ed. J. F. Walvoord and R. B. Zuck, vol. 1 (Wheaton, IL: Victor Books, 1985), 229.
2. Kendell H. Easley, *Holman QuickSource Guide to Understanding the Bible* (Nashville: Holman Bible, 2002), 43.

Day 11 | Ruth: Refuge in the Kinsman-Redeemer

1. Marvin A. Sweeney and Mark Allan Powell, "Naomi," in *The HarperCollins Bible Dictionary*, revised and updated, ed. Mark Allan Powell (New York: Harper-Collins, 2011), 688–89.
2. Jonathan Prime, *Opening up Ruth*, Opening Up Commentary (Leominster, England: Day One, 2007), 79–80.
3. Norman L. Geisler and Thomas A. Howe, *When Critics Ask: A Popular Handbook on Bible Difficulties* (Wheaton, IL: Victor Books, 1992), 153.
4. Kellie's response to this question originated from an answer she heard Rick Warren give to a similar question regarding the pandemic crisis. For a clip of that interview, visit https://www.cnn.com/videos/us/2020/04/10/where-is-god -in-pandemic-crisis-faith-rick-warren-intv-town-hall-vpx.cnn.

Day 12 | David: When Life Takes a Turn

1. Many scholars agree that the complete fulfillment of the Davidic covenant will occur during the millennial reign of Christ, when Jesus returns to establish his kingdom on earth and into eternity. For the purposes of our study, we will focus on the bloodline of David and the eternal aspect of the prophecy.
2. Walter A. Elwell and Barry J. Beitzel, "David," in *Baker Encyclopedia of the Bible* (Grand Rapids: Baker, 1988), 586.
3. David Limbaugh, *The Emmaus Code: Finding Jesus in the Old Testament* (Washington, DC: Regnery, 2015), 111.

Day 13 | Josiah: Life in Dry Seasons

1. Thomas L. Constable, "1 Kings," in *The Bible Knowledge Commentary: An Exposition of the Scriptures*, ed. J. F. Walvoord and R. B. Zuck, vol. 1 (Wheaton, IL: Victor Books, 1985), 499.

NOTES

2. H. D. M. Spence-Jones, ed., *2 Kings*, The Pulpit Commentary (London; New York: Funk & Wagnalls, 1909), 437.

Day 14 | *Jesse Tree: Your Story Isn't Over*

1. By "Judah," I am referring to the Southern Kingdom of Judah, to whom Isaiah was a prophet. The Northern Kingdom of Israel was conquered by Assyria in 722 BC.

2. Walter A. Elwell and Barry J. Beitzel, "Jesse, Root Of," in *Baker Encyclopedia of the Bible* (Grand Rapids: Baker, 1988), 1140–41.

3. John A. Martin, "Isaiah," in *The Bible Knowledge Commentary: An Exposition of the Scriptures*, ed. J. F. Walvoord and R. B. Zuck, vol. 1 (Wheaton, IL: Victor Books, 1985), 1056.

Day 17 | *He Will Suffer for Me*

1. Norman L. Geisler and Frank Turek, *I Don't Have Enough Faith to Be an Atheist* (Wheaton, IL: Crossway, 2004), 327–38. This story also includes details Dr. Leventhal shared during class lecture. Used with permission.

2. Spiros Zodhiates and Warren Baker, "Isaiah," in *The Complete Word Study Old Testament: Bringing the Original Text to Life* (Chattanooga: AMG, 1994).

3. Gary Smith, *Isaiah 40–66*, New American Commentary 15B (Nashville: Broadman & Holman, 2009), 450.

4. H. D. M. Spence-Jones, ed., *Isaiah*, vol. 2, The Pulpit Commentary (London; New York: Funk & Wagnalls, 1910), 297.

5. John A. Martin, "Isaiah," in *The Bible Knowledge Commentary: An Exposition of the Scriptures*, ed. J. F. Walvoord and R. B. Zuck, vol. 1 (Wheaton, IL: Victor Books, 1985), 1109.

Day 19 | *New Covenant: Change Is Coming*

1. Charles H. Dyer, "Jeremiah," in *The Bible Knowledge Commentary: An Exposition of the Scriptures*, ed. J. F. Walvoord and R. B. Zuck, vol. 1 (Wheaton, IL: Victor Books, 1985), 1172.

2. Alfred Edersheim, *The Life and Times of Jesus the Messiah*, vol. 2 (New York: Longmans, Green, 1896), 611.

NOTES

3. Edersheim, *Life and Times*, 611.

Day 20 | *Exile: The Fourth Man in the Fire*

1. Stephen R. Miller, *Daniel*, New American Commentary 18 (Nashville: Broadman & Holman, 1994), 110.

2. Miller, *Daniel*, 123–24.

Day 21 | *Return from Exile: Strength for God's Work*

1. E. Michael Rusten and Sharon Rusten, *The Complete Book of When & Where in the Bible and Throughout History* (Wheaton, IL: Tyndale House, 2005), 46.

2. John A. Martin, "Ezra," in *The Bible Knowledge Commentary: An Exposition of the Scriptures*, ed. J. F. Walvoord and R. B. Zuck, vol. 1 (Wheaton, IL: Victor Books, 1985), 662.

3. Mervin Breneman, *Ezra, Nehemiah, Esther*, New American Commentary 10 (Nashville: Broadman & Holman, 1993), 139.

Day 22 | *Mary: Delivering His Message*

1. Trent C. Butler, *Luke*, Holman New Testament Commentary 3 (Nashville: Broadman & Holman, 2000), 22.

2. Robert B. Hughes and J. Carl Laney, *Tyndale Concise Bible Commentary*, Tyndale Reference Library (Wheaton, IL: Tyndale House, 2001), 443–44.

Day 23 | *Shepherds: Following the Savior*

1. Robert H. Stein, *Luke*, New American Commentary 24 (Nashville: Broadman & Holman, 1992), 109.

2. M. G. Easton, *Illustrated Bible Dictionary and Treasury of Biblical History, Biography, Geography, Doctrine, and Literature* (New York: Harper & Brothers, 1893), 142.

3. Trent C. Butler, *Luke*, Holman New Testament Commentary 3 (Nashville: Broadman & Holman, 2000), 29.

Day 24 | *Wise Men: Rejoicing with Great Joy*

1. Jessica Evans, "Preparing for the August 2017 Total Solar Eclipse," NASA, December 14, 2016, https://www.nasa.gov/solar-system/preparing-for-the-august-2017-total-solar-eclipse.

NOTES

2. Stuart K. Weber, *Matthew*, Holman New Testament Commentary 1 (Nashville: Broadman & Holman, 2000), 20.

3. Weber, *Matthew*, 19.

4. Louis A. Barbieri Jr., "Matthew," in *The Bible Knowledge Commentary: An Exposition of the Scriptures*, ed. J. F. Walvoord and R. B. Zuck, vol. 2 (Wheaton, IL: Victor Books, 1985), 22.

Day 25 | *Living in the Light of Jesus*

1. Kenneth O. Gangel, *John*, Holman New Testament Commentary 4 (Nashville: Broadman & Holman, 2000), 161.

Appendix B: *The Origin of the Jesse Tree*

1. Michael J. Wilcock, "1 and 2 Chronicles," in *New Bible Commentary: 21st Century Edition*, ed. D. A. Carson et al., 4th ed. (Leicester, England; Downers Grove, IL: Inter-Varsity Press, 1994), 391.

2. F. L. Cross and Elizabeth A. Livingstone, eds., *The Oxford Dictionary of the Christian Church* (Oxford; New York: Oxford University Press, 2005), 875.

ABOUT THE AUTHOR

DONNA AMIDON is a wife, mom, speaker, musician, and lover of all things Bible. She is a graduate of Southern Evangelical Seminary and has dedicated herself to engaging women in the rich truths of Scripture while weaving its application into daily life. With a passion for the local church, Donna has served as a Bible teacher, worship leader, radio broadcaster, small groups director, and pastor's wife.

Currently, Donna homeschools her two children and is an active speaker for Stonecroft Ministries and various women's events. In addition to speaking, Donna teaches at Back to the Bible, hosting short video programs to encourage Christians in their spiritual journeys.

Donna and her husband of twenty-three years reside in Virginia with their two teenage children. Connect with Donna on Instagram (@donnaamidon_) and Facebook at Ignite the Heart, or say hello at www.donnaamidon.org. She'd love to hear from you.